THE
WHITE MOUSE

THE AUTOBIOGRAPHY
OF THE WOMAN THE GESTAPO CALLED

THE
WHITE MOUSE

NANCY WAKE

First published by Sun Books 1986
THE MACMILLAN COMPANY OF AUSTRALIA PTY LTD
107 Moray Street, South Melbourne 3205
6 Clarke Street, Crows Nest 2065

Associated companies and representatives
throughout the world

National Library of Australia
cataloguing in publication data

Wake, Nancy, 1912–
    The autobiography of the woman the Gestapo called the
    White Mouse.

    Includes index,
    ISBN 0 7251 0523 2 (pbk.).

    1. Wake, Nancy, 1912–   . 2. World War, 1939–1945–
    Underground movements – France. 3. World War, 1939–1945
    – Personal narratives, Australian, I. Title. II. Title:
    The White Mouse.

940.53′44′0924

Set in Garamond by ProComp Productions Pty Ltd, Adelaide
Printed in Hong Kong

CONTENTS

Prologue   vi

Part One

    Chapter One   1
    Chapter Two   6

Part Two

    Chapter Three   25
    Chapter Four   35
    Chapter Five   45
    Chapter Six   54
    Chapter Seven   71

Part Three

    Chapter Eight   101
    Chapter Nine   114
    Chapter Ten   157

Part Four

    Chapter Eleven   169
    Chapter Twelve   182

Index   201

PROLOGUE

29 February, 1944:

As the Liberator bomber circled over the dropping zone in France I could see lights flashing and huge bonfires burning. I hoped the field was manned by the Resistance and not by German ambushers. Huddled in the belly of the bomber, airsick and vomiting, I was hardly Hollywood's idea of a glamorous spy. I probably looked grotesque.

Over civilian clothes, silk-stockinged and high-heeled, I wore overalls, carried revolvers in the pockets, and topped the lot with a bulky camel-haired coat, webbing harness, parachute and tin hat. Even more incongruous was the matronly handbag, full of cash and secret instructions for D-day. My ankles were bandaged for support when I hit the ground.

But I'd spent years in France working as an escape courier. I'd walked out across the Pyrenees and joined the Special Operations Executive in England, and I was desperate to return to France and continue working against Hitler. Neither airsickness nor looking like a clumsily wrapped parcel was going to deter me.

The reception field in operation that night was too small for the arrival of two agents. My co-saboteur, Hubert, jumped first. By the time I landed, my parachute had drifted over to the adjacent field, and I landed in a thick hedge. My parachute was tangled in a tree.

Everything around me was dark and silent. I couldn't see any lights or fires. I quickly detached myself from my parachute, removed the bandages from my ankles, took off my overalls and ran away to crouch behind some bushes.

Then I heard Hubert's voice in the distance and someone else said, 'Here's the parachute.' I ran towards them and forced myself through a hedge to find myself face to face with a good-looking young Frenchman. Being typically French he proceeded to make some very gallant remarks: 'I hope all trees in France bear such beautiful fruit this year.' I took this with a grain of salt. After all, I had lived in France for ten years, and was married to a Frenchman.

However, he scored the first point. He refused to let me bury my parachute, which I'd been trained emphatically to do without fail. Once he had retrieved it he folded it up very neatly and put it under his arm. (Much later, sleeping in the forest, I was grateful for those nylon sheets.)

The Frenchman's name was Henri Tardivat and we were destined to become life-long friends.

Relieved that we'd landed safely, Hubert and I were whisked off alomst immediately to a little village where we were to stay at the home of some friendly Resistance people until our contact arrived.

Two mornings later my hostess invited me for a stroll around the village. It was a beautiful sunny day so I accepted. Hubert had not recovered from the strain of the previous forty-eight hours and he declined the invitation to accompany us. I was relieved he stayed behind, as it soon became apparent the whole village knew about the parachutage from beginning to end. However, they had only expected one agent and when a second one turned up, and a woman into the bargain, it was more than our hosts could stand. Hence the stroll!

Having lived in France since before the beginning of the war, I understood how these incidents could occur during the Occupation. Security-conscious Hubert would have been horrified to see me standing in the village square, shaking hands with the entire population. Nevertheless my old 'brain box' was already thinking of ways and means to find a safe house as soon as formalities would allow.

The point was that during the Occupation the majority of people (unless of course they supported the Germans) got such a thrill when something good for the cause happened they would simply let their exuberance overcome their sense of security. I did not mention my unofficial reception to Hubert at the time as I did not want to depress him any further. Our arrival and the fanfare which followed had been the direct opposite to any of the exercises included in our training programme in England. Hubert was also having language trouble, as his otherwise excellent French was too academically pure for easy conversation with these country people. Secretly I sympathised with him but I also believed we should not overlook the fact that we were strangers here and that our own reactions in the first vital days would be repeated by word of mouth, and our behaviour quickly summed up by the French people we were hoping to work closely with.

It was easier for me. I had witnessed the Occupation from its inception. Furthermore, I had lived in the country so long I could think like them and feel instinctively how they would react to certain situations. In a nutshell, I was French, except by birth.

PART ONE

CHAPTER ONE

This is the story of a naive and rather sensitive young Australasian romantic who arrived in Paris in 1934 determined not to be uncouth, and of how her experiences made her the woman who K.O.'d a waiter with her bare fist in a Paris club in 1945.

I was born in Wellington, New Zealand, in 1912. Both my parents were New Zealanders but our family settled in Sydney, Australia, when I was about two years old.

As a child I had always dreamt of seeing the world and in particular New York, London and Paris. Then one sunny day in December, 1932, my dreams became reality and I sailed out of Sydney Harbour on my way to Vancouver, New York and Europe. I still remember the feeling of exhilaration that ran through me as I stood on the deck looking out to sea and wondering what the future had in store for me.

I found New York to be an exciting city and in retrospect I think I was very fortunate not to get into too much strife because I certainly went to places that were dangerous even in those days. Prohibition was in full swing but I had never consumed so much alcohol in my short life. People used to make it in bath tubs. I was young and my liver was in good shape but when I sailed from New York my voice was decidedly hoarse.

We docked at Liverpool. It was a gloomy, foggy day and the city looked dirty and black. As the boat train slipped into London I looked through the window and there again the city was dark, gloomy and foggy.

I went to live in a cheap boarding house and enrolled in a college specialising in journalism. I hoped this profession would also be a means of travelling.

The months flew by in London. I grew to love the city and made many friends. Europe was in the throes of a depression

1

and although my friends were struggling to make ends meet we were a cheerful, happy-go-lucky crowd and we enjoyed life to the full. Somehow or other, in between studying and pub crawls, I managed to see something of the countryside and when I at last obtained a job in Paris I was almost sorry to leave England.

Although I was ecstatic to be working in Paris I was also very worried about my job. I had been taken more or less on six months' trial as a freelance reporter. As it turned out I became friendly with some of the older journalists and they never failed to help me with their good advice. I owe them all a debt of gratitude.

There was something magical about living in Paris in those days. Parisians would tell me how wonderful the city had been before and after the Great War—'la Belle Epoque', as they called it—but to me it was the most glorious place in the world and I adored working and living there.

I always feel that Paris is a woman's city, full of thrills, intrigues, gaiety, beautiful clothes and beautiful jewellery. Life there can be so exciting and amusing, but it can also teach one to appreciate things of value. In all the years I have known Paris I have never tired of wandering along the boulevards, sometimes window-shopping and frequently discovering something new, perhaps a little side street or an alleyway. This is one of the delights of Paris. It is full of surprises. Just to sit on the terrace of a café and watch the crowds pass by is in itself an entertainment.

I stayed at the Hôtel Scribe for several days when I first arrived, then went hunting for accommodation. Through a French acquaintance I was given an address in the rue Sainte-Anne and to my delight the concierge had known an Australian soldier after World War I and she had never forgotten him. It may have been a case of reflected glory as I became the tenant of a tiny flat on top of the building. I was in seventh heaven. There was no bathroom but she let me put a bath in the kitchen, and forever afterwards in the *quartier* I was known as the mademoiselle with the bath.

I learnt to shop in the little markets scattered around Paris.

I learnt to appreciate my food and wine and, better still, learnt to cook. Even today nothing would give me greater pleasure than to prepare a dish or a meal for someone who appreciates fine food, but alas, outside Europe and especially France, connoisseurs are few and far between.

At twenty-two, my life in Paris was carefree once I realised that with the help of my more experienced journalist friends, I could make a living. I wrote articles and did interviews, and sold them to press agencies, mostly the Americans. Travel was cheap, and we used to sniff around the country, usually by train, in the hope of an article. Rents were low, and paid twice-yearly. Although those two payments caused some sleepless nights, for the rest of the year all my money could be spent as frivolously as I cared to. Although I was much younger than most of my friends I enjoyed their company and I know they enjoyed mine. When I was young I did not mix easily with people of my own age. Most evenings we would congregate on the terrace of one of several cafés we patronised. Money was scarce but whenever one of us had a windfall we would share our good fortune and have a good meal with several bottles of wine followed by a *pousse-café* if the purse strings would stretch that far.

Shortly after Hitler came to power in 1933 more and more Germans were attempting to leave their country, either officially or unofficially, and thousands of those who succeeded in doing so came to Paris. There the majority hoped to obtain a visa for England, America or Canada. The ones I met were mostly academics and intellectuals, and many of them were Jews. We became friendly with several of the refugees and our little group expanded until we occupied several tables. Hitler had assumed the title of Reich Chancellor in 1933, and one of our new friends had been a Socialist member of parliament and was an escapee from that regime. He gave us first-hand information on the political side of life under the Nazis. He was fortunate enough to receive a visa for one of the South American countries. We managed to give him a great farewell party and literally poured him on to his boat train.

A group of us decided to go and see for ourselves, and in 1934 we went to Vienna, hoping to be able to sell some articles when we got back. That trip was an important one for me, for it was in Vienna that I saw several groups of Jews being persecuted. I was horrified and revolted by the public scenes.

People have often asked me how I came to work against the Germans. It was easy. It was in Vienna that I formed my own opinion of the Nazis. I resolved there and then that if I ever had the chance I would do anything, however big or small, stupid or dangerous, to try and make things more difficult for their rotten party. When war came to France, followed by the Occupation, I found it quite natural to take the stand I did.

Some time after visiting Vienna, I went with a group of journalists to Berlin. The Brownshirts were evrywhere. I remember one great fat Stormtrooper strutting around cracking a whip on the side of his long leather boots and alternately screaming and whipping at the Jewish shopkeepers. At the same time some of his colleagues painted the word 'Jew' in red paint on the windows and doors of the shops, and others threw out the contents to create huge bonfires.

I felt sick witnessing such violence. I wanted to leave the city immediately. More than hatred or anger, I felt a deep loathing for the Nazis. I had never been interested in politics and although probably leaning towards being agnostic, I had always believed in freedom of religion and worship, so I was horrified to witness so many examples of the outcome of Hitler's policies.

Back in Paris I would think of all the chaos in Germany. But what could an inexperienced girl like myself do or hope to achieve when so many brilliant well-informed men had failed to make an impact on the outside world? Although by spring 1934 over 60,000 Germans had left their country, no one wanted to hear their stories of the New Germany. The majority of politicians and their leaders all behaved like ostriches whenever the subject of Hitler was broached. Alas, very soon the world was forced to admit the existence of a new word—GESTAPO—but it was too late and by the time the

4

people took their heads out of the sand hundreds of thousands of innocent people had been slaughtered. My visits to Vienna and Berlin had sobered me, but back in Paris the old life continued. Two important characters now entered my life: Picon and Stephanie.

CHAPTER TWO

Falling in love was bound to happen sooner or later. For many months I had been free to come and go as I pleased in the little flat in rue Sainte-Anne. I was in the habit of taking a brisk morning walk through the Tuileries whenever possible; not that I was a lover of exercise. However, I felt the clean fresh air counteracted to some extent the thick smoky haze of the previous nights.

One day I crossed over to the rue de Rivoli, intending to window-gaze. Suddenly I had one of those queer sensations one can get at times. I looked, and there he was. Our eyes met and I hesitated for a second and walked quickly away. But something pulled me back and I stood staring at him for a few minutes. It was love at first sight for us both. I entered the shop and came out the proud owner of a wire-haired terrier barely three weeks old.

He was named Picon by the barman at Luigi's. A visiting clergyman from the States gave a short address and I promised to bring him up as a law-abiding citizen. We were inseparable companions. The concierge adored him, so did all my friends, and very soon he was a much loved guest of the many eating and drinking establishments I patronised. At night when I was ready to go out I'd say, 'Picon, do you want to make the *bombe?*' and he would rush to the door, ready to do the rounds of all the places in vogue at that time. Friends seeing him the day after would be able to make a rough guess as to what time I had retired the night before. After a night on the tiles Picon would just lie down and sleep anywhere, until it was time to start all over again.

Then Stephanie came to stay.

I was going to Marseille in October 1934, hoping to write an article on the visit there of King Alexander of Yugoslavia. As the Paris Express pulled into Cannes, I saw the most extraordinarily beautiful young woman standing on the platform with an older man. Later, they appeared in the restaurant car.

I was intrigued, but soon forgot them. At Marseille, I booked into the Hôtel du Louvre et Paix, and explored the city on foot before the procession began.

I wandered up and down the narrow alleys and passageways, sometimes peering into the courtyards or casting a glance at the prostitutes plying their trade. Strangely enough, I have never been afraid in Marseille. In later years I was destined to know it well and I would walk alone in the most insalubrious areas.

As I retraced my footsteps to the Vieux Port I could smell the saffron in the air—the little bistros and restaurants were preparing their fish soups and bouillabaisse. It was early yet but the spicy warm odour of the saffron was too much for me and I entered a small bistro right on the Port, took a seat at a table on the terrace and ordered the only aperitif possible in Marseille before bouillabaisse, a pastis. It was a fine, pleasant day and I soon began to feel that life was really worthwhile. The meal was excellent and I washed it down with a bottle of my favourite rosé, a Tavel. Louis XVI and I certainly had something in common, I told myself as I finished the wine.

I made my way to the Canebière and took up my position on the steps of the Bourse to watch the King go by. The crowds began to cheer as the carriage approached but then came the sound of shots being fired. Someone shouted that they had shot the King, and then all hell broke loose.

Marseille crowds are never very orderly when things are normal, but let someone loose with a gun and they become more dangerous than the person with the gun. I put on a performance that would have done credit to an Olympic runner and reached my hotel in record time. I headed for the American bar, which I guessed would be a pleasant enough corner in which to take up a defensive position.

The lobby of the hotel was seething with people running all over the place, but all was calm in the bar as the head barman looked after the requests of his clients. I rang through to Paris with my story as soon as a line was available and then proceeded to enjoy the scene in the lobby from my stool at the bar. Police were everywhere. Everyone was shouting and waving their arms in the air. I had already noticed in France that it was generally the person who shouted the loudest who

7

won the floor. It had absolutely nothing to do with being right or wrong. Nevertheless, this spirit appealed to my exuberant nature.

Very soon the police shouted for me. My name was on the hotel register and I was a foreigner into the bargain. It's really extraordinary, but in every country in the world, foreigners are always suspected before anyone else.

The barman had looked after me exceedingly well and I felt sure I could cope with the situation. Besides, I had experienced months of shouting in Paris and no Marseille *flic* was going to outshout me. After a short session of witty repartee the policeman calmed down and dismissed me with a snort. Since arriving in France I'd learnt my French by trial and error. Making mistakes is the best way to learn—you're determined not to make the same mistake again.

The barman was impressed by my performance and insisted on buying me a drink, then I bought him one and then all the staff on the ground floor joined in the fun, until the scene was reminiscent of a Marx brothers' comedy. By this time we had been told that the King was dead and that a French cabinet minister who had been travelling with him in the carriage was either dead or dying.

From that point on things became a little blurred but somewhere along the line the beautiful woman from the train appeared in the bar, where she had a terrible row with her companion and threw a jug of iced water over his disappearing figure. I was the only one remaining in the bar besides the barman (the others having fled when the row started) and she proceeded to tell me the story of her life. If this had happened a few hours previously I might have been interested, but French hospitality had taken its toll and all I wanted to do was sleep. Anywhere. However, I did gather that she was Yugoslavian and had just returned from South America with her husband, who was very jealous. And her name was Stephanie.

Before I could withdraw or retire to my room the husband reappeared. There was another discussion between the two and after bursting into tears they both hugged each other. The barman and I were both spellbound. We were just about to congratulate the couple on their reconciliation when, with a scream worthy of a fish wife, Stephanie threw the only remaining jug of iced water at her husband.

This left me with a fresh glass of Ricard and no iced water, and I expressed my displeasure in no uncertain terms, whereupon she let fly at me in a French that was new to me. It was a formidable and enlightening performance because very little she mentioned was in my dictionary or my book of French phrases for the tourist. Then abruptly she left her husband standing in the bar, soaking wet, and swept out through the lobby towards the door, only to be stopped by a policeman who demanded to see her papers.

The policeman was indeed fortunate that there were no more water jugs at hand; as it was, Stephanie hit him on the head with her handbag (and they were large that year) then disappeared through the revolving doors followed closely by the red-faced policeman. Her husband checked out of the hotel with his suitcase half an hour later. The barman and I just looked at each other; we could not believe it had all happened. My sleepiness had gone. We had just settled down when in swept Stephanie, escorted by the policeman with whom she had disappeared. They both looked calm and he bowed as he put her in the lift.

The drama was becoming too farcical for words when down came Stephanie looking for her husband. He had gone. He had taken her at her word and left for a warmer clime. I feared the situation might never improve and decided the only safe place for me in my state was in bed behind a locked door. After all, it had been a very long day. I awoke with the dawn. I had been dreaming I was dying of thirst and it was not long before I realised I was not well enough to think about the events of the previous day so I determined to put them out of my head for twenty-four hours. I also decided to take the first express train to Paris as that might give me enough time to recuperate and get over the shock of the Latin farce.

I said goodbye to all the staff, promising to come back whenever I could. (I kept my promise and when I married in 1939 the reception was held at the Hôtel du Louvre et Paix.)

I settled down in a window seat in an empty compartment, and slept for hours. When I awoke for a few seconds I thought I was dreaming. Sitting by the corridor diagonally opposite was Stephanie. I shut my eyes quickly and tried to gather my thoughts. There was no doubt about it, I would have to find another seat. But when I showed signs of moving she came over and apologised for her bad behaviour, adding that she had been a little upset. As far as I was concerned that was the understatement of the year but when I was young I was of a forgiving nature. Before very long we adjourned to the restaurant car for some refreshment as we were both a little under the weather. It was the beginning of a long and deep friendship which although hectic in varying degrees was never dull or boring. She made me familiar with a side of life I had never before encountered and I always held for her a special affection.

By the time I had reached Paris I had invited her to stay with me until she could find a place of her own, and as she had no friends in the capital she was happy to accept my invitation. We got on very well in the little flat. She was fun to live with and had lots of good points. She was scrupulously clean and tidy, always willing to do her share of the work, but best of all she had a delightful sense of fun.

We both loved our food and we liked cooking but we seldom ate at home. We were young and full of the joys of spring. Life was cheap in Paris and in any case we were never short of escorts. Nevertheless, I had resolved to keep her away from my journalist friends. I was enjoying my job and our shared activities, and every time I thought of Stephanie let loose amongst them I would get cold shivers up and down my spine.

When I was free Stephanie and I would arrange a foursome and do the rounds of the amusing restaurants and go on to a cabaret or night-club. Sometimes just the two of us would go to a music hall or theatre. There was so much to do in Paris that winter. Mistinguette was in a revue at the Folies-Bergère and Cecile Sorel was opening at the Casino de Paris in a revue for the first time after having been with the Comédie Française for over thirty years. Josephine Baker was on the scene; so was Jean Sablon, who made all the girls swoon with his hit, 'Je tire ma reverence'. I met Harry Bauer and he invited us to *The Trial of Oscar Wilde*, in which he was playing the lead. We sobbed all through his performance and when he took us to supper at La Rue after the show we were still weeping.

Stephanie was always falling in love. I was not in love with anyone in particular so I was not going through the agonies most young lovers do. I was in love with life but most of all I was in love with Paris. I learnt how to make *pastis* and we turned a little corner in the kitchen into our distillery. The strong odour of aniseed wafted out to the courtyard, but the concierge loved our brew and was more than delighted to watch us swindle the government out of a few francs in tax.

I was enjoying the best of two worlds—my journalist friends on one hand, and my French friends and Stephanie on the other. I went on working, and I went on having fun. I was not to know then that the ease with which I could run two or more parallel lives successfully would be useful later. Similarly, my train and bus trips around France on assignment gave me a familiarity with provincial public transport which was important on more dangerous trips in the future.

The intrigues within Spain at this time extended to their embassy in Paris and a variety of strange Spaniards could be seen calling on their officials, although it was not easy to identify them. Actually, some of them were so flamboyant it was hard to take them seriously. As in any big city gradually filling with refugees, and with impending disaster in the air, Paris was full of rumours. At times it was difficult to know what to believe. However, a fairly reliable source informed our little group of journalists that several Spaniards were involved in smuggling arms and ammunition from France into Spain. Furthermore, according to our informant, certain officials in the French Government were well aware of these activities.

A scoop like this was bound to interest any journalist so three of us left immediately for Biarritz where we were friendly with a knowledgeable local businessman. It turned out to be a wild goose chase, although some months later we were convinced there had been a lot of truth in the rumour.

I had a good friend in Tarbes who had been involved in tobacco smuggling for years, and I was not in a hurry to return to Paris. I decided to pay her a visit, hoping she could give me a lead on the illegal traffic that was obviously going on between the two countries. I took a bus to Pau passing through very beautiful countryside. At Pau I resisted the temptation to visit Lourdes, a decision that was to have some significance years later when I was arrested in Toulouse, and

11

could truthfully say I had never been to Lourdes.

I wandered around the town for a couple of hours waiting for my connection, then sat on the terrace of a bistro. I could see the spectacular Pyrenees from there. Little did I know that a few years later I would know those mountains better.

My trip to Tarbes was a success. My friend introduced me to a Spanish Nationalist who appeared to be heavily involved in many Spanish intrigues. As in Paris we were anxious to obtain first-hand information on the political situation I felt he might prove useful to our little circle of journalists.

Shortly after my return to Paris I paid another visit to Vienna, where there had been a steady deterioration of the political situation. There were endless strikes, street demonstrations, police violence and, worst of all, Austrian denouncing Austrian. Inflation was ruining the economy. Previously Vienna had resembled Paris in many ways, but now it was just another city where fear had swept into the lives of the people. Like London it had been a paradise for the eccentric, but now it was fast becoming a hell on earth for all who were not Nazis. The fortunate ones escaped and some of them came to Paris, but as always with the Gestapo countless innocent citizens fell victim to their atrocities. Every year Paris would be filled with rich tourists from all parts of the globe, and the spring and early summer of 1935 was no exception, but now it was not unusual to see little groups of refugees huddled together on the café terraces. They contributed a little more to the already cosmopolitan air of the city.

My admiration for these refugees from Germany and Austria grew and I would seek out their company. I have always been a good listener and those years were interesting and informative ones for me. I was able to hear the views of some brilliant men, experienced in the ways of life. Irrespective of their background they were united by their principles. They accepted me because I too believed in freedom. I was young but I already knew the horrors a totalitarian state could bring, and long before the Second World War was declared I also understood that a free world can only remain free by defending itself against any form of aggression. I knew too that freedom could not be permanent. It has to be defended at all cost, even

12

if by doing so part of our freedom has to be sacrificed. It will always be in danger because, alas, victory is not permanent.

In August 1935, most people who could leave the city were making for the sea, the mountains or the country. My holidays were due and Stephanie was taking me to her home near a little village about eighty kilometres inland from Split in Yugoslavia. As far as I know I was the first friend of hers to visit her parents, and I was looking forward to meeting them. I knew from Stephanie that they were a simple peasant couple and I had always wondered how they could have produced such an exotic creature.

We travelled south on the Blue Train, shopping and visiting friends for two days, then, went on to Split and wandered around exploring before catching our bus into the country. Soon after we arrived at the little whitewashed cottage. Stephanie's mother came in from the fields to greet us. She hugged her daughter several times and shook hands with me but never once gave either of us a welcoming smile. I was frankly amazed at her appearance. I knew she had to work hard so I was prepared for wrinkled and gnarled hands, but she was so unlike her daughter it was hard to believe they were of the same family.

Stephanie was the most magnificent creature I had ever seen. I have never known anyone so beautiful. She had large, slightly almond shaped eyes the colour of the deepest blue hydrangea, soft golden hair with a natural wave, dimples in her cheeks and a tall willowy figure which never varied in weight one single ounce.

Stephanie was anxious to show me all over the cottage where she had been born. We went out to the well where as a child she had drawn the water; the stream where she had washed the clothes; the cellar where they distilled their slivovitz (plum brandy) and where she had stolen her first tipple. It was with positive pride she pointed out the fields scattered around the immediate area where they grew their crops. The kitchen was enormous and it contained the largest kitchen table I have ever seen. It must have been assembled in the room as it would have been impossible to put it through the doors or windows. It was scrubbed twice daily and was spotlessly clean. There was a big black pot dangling on the end

13

of a long chain fastened to the top of the chimney. Underneath, a fire was slowly burning, and the most delicious aroma was filling the kitchen.

That evening we sat down to a table laden with food. The Yugoslavs have absorbed into their own national cooking many dishes from neighbouring countries and when I saw the assortment of food I knew why Stephanie had such an enormous appetite. Everything they consumed was grown or produced on their land. On the table were tiny skinless pork sausages, meat patties made with pork and veal, several dishes of assorted vegetables, some in brine and some in oil, field mushrooms marinated in oil and herbs, a funny kind of home-made bread which was flat and spongy and was excellent for mopping up sauce, a huge smoked ham which one of the daughters cut in thin slices, smoked eels, poached river fish in sauce and a large mound of butter wrapped in vine leaves.

Then along came a chicken soup with herbs that were strange to me and thickened with egg yolk and sour cream. In between courses we downed small glasses of slivovitz to aid our digestion and with our food we drank lashings of local wine. Stephanie's mother hovered around the table making sure we had enough to eat, but never once did she or her husband exchange a word. The rest of the family, Stephanie's brother and two sisters were boisterous. The big black pot was pulled over from the hearth and placed on a wooden stool next to the table, and the mother served us each in turn as we passed our plates. It contained an assortment of green, yellow and red peppers, stuffed with minced pork, veal, beef, rice, mushrooms, parsley, cheese and herbs. They had been simmering all day in a delicious sauce made with pounds of tomatoes, onions, garlic, paprika, herbs and white wine. I had never tasted anything like it in my life and I made a mental note to lock Stephanie in the kitchen when we returned to Paris.

We finished the meal by drinking thick, sweet black coffee which should not be stirred because of the sediment in the cup. Then more slivovitz in an effort to make room for the assorted pastries which followed.

When the rest of the family had retired for the night Stephanie and I gave the bottle of slivovitz another little nudge and I asked her why her parents did not speak to each

14

other. She replied quite casually that they all hated their father so much that no one bothered to talk to him unless it was absolutely necessary. When he drank to excess he became violent. He had broken her mother's jaw and smashed her teeth during one session, and this was the reason she never smiled or spoke in front of strangers. Stephanie had offered to pay for her mother's dental treatment many times but the poor woman was petrified at the thought of a dentist and so remained toothless until she died. The children adored their mother and protected her from the father as much as they could. If he so much as raised a hand to her they would beat him with the first available weapon. I was not surprised that this had made him bitter and twisted.

In spite of this extraordinary domestic situation I enjoyed my holiday with Stephanie's family. It was unbelievably cold but sometimes if the sun was warm we would sit outside in the middle of the day. The cottage was surrounded by olive groves and hundreds of grape vines which seemed to grow in rocky soil. Several nights we roasted a whole lamb on a spit outside the kitchen door and ate it with our fingers. If Stephanie dropped a piece on the ground she just picked it up and ate it but she always swallowed a drop of slivovitz afterwards, being a firm believer in this beverage and maintaining it was also a good disinfectant.

We were both sad when we had to leave. Having seen Stephanie at home with her family I felt I could understand her complex nature more than I had before. To my surprise her mother took me in her arms, kissed me on both cheeks and made me promise to return. A promise I could not fulfil, as the war on the horizon changed the destiny of each of us.

Paris was looking beautiful when I returned from my holiday and it was fun to meet my friends again and catch up with the news. The contact to whom I had been introduced in Tarbes was due to arrive any day and we were looking forward to receiving the latest news of the conflict in Spain.

While I'd been away the most extraordinary man had appeared at our favourite café and cottoned himself on to our little group. He had an aristocratic-sounding name but we all called him Count Gonzales. He was good-looking, tall and slim with thick wavy black hair. Although he was Spanish he had a fair complexion and hazel eyes, which was most unusual. Unlike us, he appeared to have money to burn. He was flamboyant and always dramatised the topic of conversation. We did not take him seriously but we found him entertaining with his stories of intrigue, smuggling, crime and even would-be murder.

Gonzales appeared to know everyone in the limelight at the time and we concluded he was either extremely well connected or the world's biggest liar. It was not long before he tried to engage me as his courier, promising me a huge salary which he increased every time the offer was renewed. There was never the slightest chance I would accept the job as I only felt safe with Gonzales when surrounded by dozens of people and the bright lights of Paris. Anyhow, I only spoke about twenty words of Spanish.

Our contact from Tarbes duly arrived. We were all sitting in the café listening to the latest and alarming news from Spain when Gonzales sauntered in and sat down at our table. Our new friend looked at him and instantly changed the subject. It was some time before we could get rid of Gonzales without making it too obvious, but when we did we were not at all surprised to be told that he was suspected of taking money from both political sides in Spain and that he could not be trusted under any circumstances. After a reasonable interval we found another meeting place and saw very little of Gonzales, but he was not a fool and probably realised we had been warned about his shady activities.

On the whole they were a mixed bunch from Spain and not all of them inspired confidence. The politicians amongst them seemed to be on both sides of the fence. Others were obviously professional smugglers and guides. They would sit in the cafés discussing the problems in Spain and offering their own particular solution until the early hours of the morning, when they would disappear into thin air. There were certainly others of a more serious nature but I seldom met them.

1936 would bring four significant events. In March, Hitler remilitarised the Rhineland without any reaction from England or France. It was several months before British Prime Minister Baldwin admitted his error in not giving credibility to Germany's rearmament. The Deuxième Bureau were equally aware of the German rearmament but seemed powerless to put their knowledge to the benefit of France, no doubt because their country was riddled with French collaborators in high places, already in the pay of the Germans.

In May, Italy annexed Abyssinia. The Popular Front won the elections in France and the threat of the Spanish Civil War became a reality in July.

Early in 1936, I was going to London for a week and invited Stephanie to come with me. She spoke six languages but not one word of English. In all the years I knew her she never expressed any desire to see England or learn the language. She refused my invitation point blank, saying, 'Ma petite, with all the men in Europe, why would I go to England where they [the men] are so cold and correct?' So both England and Englishmen missed a golden opportunity to show her that things could be otherwise. Looking back, I can see that Stephanie would have made some psychiatrist very happy. She was such a complex person with some very unorthodox views. Little by little I was able to piece together some parts of the life she led after she first married and before we both met, but it was not very easy and I found myself writing little notes whenever any new clues came to light. Ours was a wonderful friendship, and although we were complete opposites in many ways I don't think I have ever laughed so much as I did in those days with Stephanie.

Some time after her first husband divorced her Stephanie married the co-respondent and went to live in Turkey, but to her dismay he left her stranded in a remote part of the country two years later. She then wrote to her first spouse, begging forgiveness. Not only did he forgive her, he took her back and married her a second time. But for ever after, if she misbehaved, he would wave her letter in her face and remind her that she had begged to be reunited. Subsequently she paid a professional letter-writer a small fee to write her love letters, so that she'd never again be trapped by evidence written in her own hand.

With tears in her eyes she would say, 'Ma petite, say what you like to them, especially on the pillow, but never put it in writing, otherwise they will get you.' A piece of advice which made me shriek with laughter.

17

Many foreigners think Paris and the Parisians are typical of France. They are not. Paris is the most beautiful city and Parisians are delightful. I love the city for all it represents and all it has given the rest of the world, just as I love Parisians for their charm, wit and culture. But there is another France as I discovered when I travelled all over the country, not as a tourist, but as one of the people.

Most visitors went first of all to Paris and then down to the Riviera, that impressive coastline stretching from Marseille to Genoa, but when I went south I went further afield off the beaten track to meet, and eventually become accepted by, people who had never seen a city, let alone Paris. During the thirties, very few tourists bothered to pass through the Camargue on their way south, which was a pity because only fifty kilometres west of Arles, once the seat of the Roman Emperor Constantine, lies the fascinating home of the French cowboys. They always look so picturesque in their cream breeches, colourful check shirts and black felt hats, riding their splendid white horses. Here too are the famous black bulls bred for the bullrings of Nîmes and Arles.

Unlike my Parisian friends, I enjoyed the provinces, and was independent enough to travel around on my own. I learnt a lot about country people, an education perhaps begun with Stephanie's family in Yugoslavia. I have always been interested in other people, how they live, what they think, but I've never been *too* curious. Looking back, it was probably my friendliness which made me accepted. Later, of course, during the war, the less you knew about your comrades the better.

The Camargue is a vast expanse of saltmarshes, wild and dramatic, with ponds and plains where herons and ibises nest, and where they can be seen wading frantically for fish. It is also a refuge for flamingoes and beavers. Sometimes you see an egret performing a kind of war dance or running around like a drunk or fluffing out its feathers at the neck, looking like a 'Beef Eater' at the Tower of London. The tall reeds of the Camargue seem to moan and groan when the Mistral sweeps down from the Rhône valley, leaving an eerie impression upon a visitor. But when the air is still and balmy, it is a mysterious place full of unexpected surprises.

Legend has it that the 'Holy Marys', Marie Jacobs and

18

Marie Salome, landed at the seaside village of Les-Saintes-Maries-de-la-Mer, with their negro servant Sarah, after having been adrift for some time on the Mediterranean. Two days have been set aside in May, the 24th and 25th, to commemorate this religious event, and a visit to the area at that time used to be well worth the effort. On the first day of the religious fête, the gypsies take the statue of their black patron saint Sarah from the church down to the sea, whence they say that she came, hoisted high on the shoulders of the believers. Camargue cowboys line the path she takes, forming a guard of honour. It is a strange sight, definitely resembling pagan times and rites. The gypsies shout 'Long live Sarah' and the priests and believers respond by shouting 'Long live the Holy Marys'.

The following day the Holy Marys are paraded down from the church to the sea supported by the priests and believers all shouting 'Long live the Holy Marys' and many 'Ave Marias', with the gypsies putting in a last good word for Sarah. It may start off by being a religious ceremony to be taken seriously, but I've been to this fête several times, and each year the unexpected has happened and the atmosphere has become hilarious.

The first year I went the gypsies became intoxicated and dropped Sarah. Then a cowboy who had started celebrating too soon passed out during the procession, tripping up a priest who was so busy singing 'Ave Maria' and raising his eyes towards the heavens that he did not notice the cowboy fall off his horse until it was too late. Another year I was invited to take part in a water sport, the name of which escapes me. One stands up in a little boat holding a long pole and another team does the same in their boat. I never did understand the rules of the game and the sea has never been my forte, so everyone ended up in the water and my team would not speak to me for ages.

I thoroughly enjoyed these little distractions at Les-Saintes-Maries-de-la-Mer, and happened to be laughing about our escapades with Stephanie not long after she had refused to go to England with me. In a flash she said we would go back the following May and nothing I said would make her change her mind.

The fête that year was unbelievably informal, to say the least. The cowboys had never seen anyone like Stephanie, even though the area has always been noted for beautiful women. But Stephanie was different. Not only was she the most beautiful woman there, but she was determined to conquer the cowboys of Camargue, even if it meant separating them from their horses.

For forty-eight hours chaos reigned. Cowboys were fighting each other, horses were shying, even the dogs seemed to be growling at each other. There were domestic problems blowing up all the time. Things went from bad to worse until finally I pretended I had not known her beforehand. I can still remember how relieved I felt to leave the village behind and arrive safely back in Paris.

When Japan attacked China in July 1937, it seemed to pass unnoticed in France, probably because the Spanish Civil War was drawing all the attention. Early that summer Stephanie and I were sitting with our boyfriends on a terrace of a café near the Madeleine when Gonzales walked by. We had not seen each other for ages as I had been avoiding him, but he came up to our table. Obviously I had to introduce him to my companions. He was delighted when Stephanie spoke to him in Spanish, and they chatted together for ages. I asked her later what they had been talking about and she replied with one word, 'Spain', which was not very informative.

Several weeks passed before friends told me she had been seen dozens of times with a tall, good-looking Spaniard. One did not have to be clever to guess that her companion was probably Gonzales. When I tackled her about the subject she told me to mind my own business. I felt as a friend I should warn her not to become too involved with him, and pass on to her the information we had been given about his suspected activities. She refused to hear one bad word against him. So I left it at that. After all, she was a grown woman who had more experience than I had, and it was her life. She became very secretive after this discussion. When eventually she told me she was going to live with Gonzales in Biarritz and act as his courier until such time as they could marry, I was almost glad to see her go. I was so worried about her plans that I actually confided in an old friend who was always willing to listen to my tales of woe, but he advised me to let well alone, pointing out that Stephanie was over twenty-one.

The flat seemed empty without her. Then out of the blue came an invitation to spend Christmas and the New Year with her in her new home, and I accepted 'post haste'. She was at the station to meet me and we went straight away to her apartment, which she was anxious for me to see. It was the most sumptuous apartment imaginable, furnished most luxuriously with everything a woman could possible desire. Gonzales was literally showering her with money. She certainly seemed very happy.

We had a wonderful Christmas and New Year. Lots of parties, dozens of guests coming and going, and I enjoyed every minute of it. Yet when at last I was on my way back to Paris I still had very grave doubts about the integrity of Gonzales. The last thing Stephanie said at the station was 'Don't worry, we'll be married soon and I'll send you a telegram.' Sure enough, the telegram arrived several weeks later.

About the following Easter I picked up a French newspaper. On the front page was the horrifying story of a bullet-riddled body picked up in a gutter in a little village on the west coast of France. Several names and aliases were mentioned though none of them meant anything to me. However, I had an ominous feeling that all was not well with Stephanie. Several weeks later she appeared on my doorstep in the middle of the night. She was very distressed and looked terrible.

The bullet-riddled body had been Gonzales. He was not dead when discovered and they had taken him to a private hospital nearby. The authorities informed several people whose names were in his diary, and Stephanie was also notified. By the time she arrived at the hospital Gonzales had been given the last rites and sacraments. Stephanie was not allowed to see him as his legal wife had arrived. He had married Stephanie bigamously.

After the initial shock of his death and her bigamous marriage there were more unpleasant surprises in store. The rent was overdue, the furniture had not been paid for and bills were piling up fast. She was left with only the clothes on her back. She had borrowed her train fare from a sympathetic barman and had come back to Paris to her only friend, as she then called me.

For hours she talked of the tragedy and the events leading up to it. I personally concluded that Gonzales had been taking money from both sides in Spain, without giving service to either one, and then eventually someone had caught up with him. It was May Day and a public holiday but I had to go to work for a short time and when I returned to my flat Stephanie was busy writing letters. I made her eat something and then she said she would try to sleep for a while. I worked on quietly for a couple of hours and then I had the strangest feeling. I crept into Stephanie's room and found her lying on the bed asleep. Then I noticed the letters she had been writing, arranged on top of the chest of drawers. I picked one up; it was addressed to the Commissioner of Police, another to her mother. I began to feel sick in the stomach. One by one I looked at the envelopes. Six letters in all, but not one to me.

I shook her violently but nothing happened. She had poisoned herself. I fled downstairs to get help. It was useless, everyone had gone out to enjoy May Day. There were no ambulances and no doctors. I raced out and phoned a young friend who lived on the other side of Paris. When he answered his phone I gave a sigh of relief as he was a final-year medical student. He told me to make her sick and he would be there as soon as he could.

By the time I returned to the flat the concierge was back. Together we mixed a concoction of everything we could think of that was handy and forced it down Stephanie's throat. Shortly afterwards the medical student arrived with a fully-fledged doctor friend of his. They both worked on Stephanie for two hours before pronouncing her to be out of danger.

Now I knew she was not going to die I was livid with rage. Had she died I would have had endless troubles as I was a foreigner, yet she had not seen fit to write me one single word. I nursed her for several days and when she was well enough I told her our friendship was over. Stephanie convinced herself that I was unreasonable and we were not on speaking terms by the time she left, not that I worried. I was also convinced I never wanted to see her again.

Three months later we met face to face in central Paris. Stephanie asked briefly if we were friends or enemies. I laughed and replied that we were friends.

22

PART TWO

CHAPTER THREE

In the 1920s the Riviera had been a fashionable winter resort attracting royalty and rich, retired conservative folk. Now it had become popular for summer holidays. All along the coast the atmosphere was one of complete and utter irresponsibility. In 1936 I decided to go to Juan les Pins for my summer holiday. It was a mad, high-spirited resort which I was sure would suit the mood I was in.

I arrived there about eight in the morning. As was usual at this time the streets were empty except for the tradesmen, workmen hosing the streets with perfumed water and the gardeners tending the beautiful little parks and flower-beds.

Some mornings a few stragglers in evening dress wending their way back to their hotels would stand daringly in front of the hoses. It was always taken in good part, amidst peals of laughter. Then suddenly the beaches would be covered with sunbathers dozing and others swimming in the lovely blue sea. Late afternoon, as soon as the warmth had gone out of the sun, the beach would become deserted and it would be the turn of the bars and cafés to be filled with light-hearted patrons consuming their aperitifs. Just as suddenly as the beach had become deserted, so would the cafés and bars as everyone wandered home to change for dinner, and then the restaurants would be the scenes of activity.

After coffee everyone would make a beeline for one of the two night-clubs that existed in Juan. Both were in the open air in romantic settings, with little tables scattered around the dance floor and low lights hidden in the branches of the trees which surrounded the entire floor. Before the night was out one could be sure that someone in each of the clubs would get up and head a long winding crocodile line and conga out into the streets, making their way to the other club.

The waiters were magnificent—handbags, furs, scarves drinks or anything left behind would be returned to the rightful owners. How they sorted out the bills I don't know, but they did. Perhaps the owners of each respective club had some secret agreement. Whatever it was, the organisation was fantastic and great fun. After a night out I used to love walking home to the hotel as the night air would be filled with the perfume of the exotic flowers, the shrubs and the trees. It was mainly a world of glittering wealth and false values; nevertheless, everyone added something to the character and charm of the resort.

That summer, I had been seeing a lot of an American who lived in Paris, and he had arranged to spend a couple of weeks at Juan les Pins while I was there. He was a fantastic dancer and enormous fun, and while we were clutched in each other's arms in the throes of a romantic tango at one of the night-clubs I happened to notice a man in the shadows who appeared to be watching every move we made. When the lights went up I saw it was a man I had met now and again at Marseille. His name was Henri Fiocca. He came over to our table and said 'Hello', and then disappeared with his companion, an attractive blonde.

The following week, my American friend returned to Paris and at the weekend who should turn up in Juan les Pins, by himself this time, but Henri Fiocca, the man from Marseille. I found he was an industrialist, and wealthy. I also found he was charming, sexy and very amusing. But I did not take him too seriously. I was too experienced to want anything but play from a playboy, and besides, I was somewhat of a playgirl myself, although of course on a much humbler economic level than Henri Fiocca. We had a wonderful time while he was there and when he left I had agreed to see him when I came south again. From then on my friends in Paris were forever ragging me unmercifully because of all the excuses I made to go south.

When I returned to Paris the news, both world-wide and local, was so depressing that I was grateful for the mad, frivolous holiday I had enjoyed in the south. In common with many others I feared war was inevitable and then where would we all be? When would laughter end and the tears begin?

The civil war in Spain was still a matter of great concern in France. Nevertheless there were countless ugly rumours of illegal and dishonest transactions going on between the two countries which in France involved prominent people. It was unfortunate that these rumours could not be confirmed at the time. Ever since the Stavisky scandals in 1933–4, when the 'greatest con-man of the century' (as he became known) was finally exposed, together with a number of influential citizens, the French people had become disenchanted with the establishment. It had become a matter of public knowledge that Stavisky and his accomplices had been guilty of a staggering number of high-powered but shady deals.

When he was exposed there was a mad rush by his associates to leave the sinking ship. To make matters worse, when he was finally run to ground near Chamonix in the Haute Savoie, his publicised 'suicide' did not convince the vast majority of French people who thought it was more likely to have been a case of murder.

Remembering all this, the man in the street did not know whom he could trust and if, indeed, he could trust anyone. When the war came, this distrust made most of the general public very cautious about becoming involved in anti-Nazi activities. A chance remark to an acquaintance who might be a collaborator would land you in a lot of trouble.

Early in 1939, Henri Fiocca asked me to marry him. The proposal came as a surprise because although we had been having a fabulous time since we had started going out regularly whenever I was in the south, I had always been aware of the reputation he had with the girls. Any time I had run into him in the past he had always been with a different girl, sometimes three or four the same day. I used to be pop-eyed at his stamina! I kept him dangling several days, remembering all the good advice my friend Stephanie had given me over the years.

Henri had arrived unexpectedly in Paris the previous November and found me surrounded by men, young and old and of several nationalities, including the American, drinking and making merry at our favourite bistro. I had introduced him to everyone and we all lunched together. He had not referred to the incident when we dined on the night he proposed, but after he had waited for my reply for several days he suddenly mentioned that day in Paris. I was absolutely stunned when this 'ladies' man' told me he was jealous and

27

hated the thought of the life I was leading in Paris. We were dining at Verduns, our favourite restaurant in Marseille. Of course I accepted after such a declaration on his part. Joseph, the *maitre d'hôtel*, was the first person to be told our exciting news and he immediately offered us a bottle of Krug champagne. There was just one hitch: old man Fiocca, Henri's father, had purchased a battleship in Toulon, hoping to sell it as scrap iron and make a fortune. Instead, the bottom fell out of the market and he lost his money. It was left to his son to put the firm back on its feet and make up the losses. Henri hoped everything would be finalised by the beginning of 1940 and asked me if I would wait until then to be married. We eventually settled for May 1940, and I stipulated that the wedding breakfast would take place at the Hôtel du Louvre et Paix.

As far as I was concerned there was another big hitch. There was no way I was going to stick to the rules of the game and pay for the wedding, and I told Henri so over the bottle of Krug. I thought Joseph would die laughing. Anyhow, I always remember Henri's reply. He said, 'Never mind, Nannie, I'll pay for it—but don't tell Papa.' As if I would. Our marriage followed the pattern we set that night at Verduns—we made our own rules, kept our mouths shut, and went on having a marvellous time.

The Spanish Civil War ended in April 1939 and General Franco took power after the murderous fighting in which a million Spaniards died. The threat of war was always hanging over Europe and it obviously had a disturbing effect on everyone. But in spite of all the apprehension we felt, our group continued to live and act as if nothing unusual was happening.

I was just living for Easter as Henri was coming to Paris. Funnily enough, now we were going to be married he didn't seem to mind all my friends, and instead of taking me away from them he seemed happy to join the circle. They all liked him, he was an amusing man and, if he liked a person, generous to a fault. We had discovered how much we enjoyed each other's company, which is quite separate from being in love. We laughed at the same things and he pretended to be long-suffering about my outspokenness. We'd both met our match and knew it.

Henri and I went to Cannes for the summer holidays in 1939. We had a wonderful time and lived for every moment. Like most people, we shut our eyes to the inevitable. We were making the most of those weeks because we were afraid that not only might it be the last summer before war, it could also be our last summer.

Cannes was very sophisticated and expensive, and it must have been one of the liveliest night spots on the Riviera. Sometimes we would walk along the Croisette past the luxury hotels on one side and the Mediterranean on the other, towards the Port. After admiring the yachts moored in the wide bay, we would choose a bistro where we would indulge in our favourite pre-lunch pastime—drinking pastis.

We went further afield to country villages and towns, and to Saint-Tropez, a typical Provençal village. Everyone dines as late as possible and crowds fill the bars or wander through the maze of narrow, twisted streets until the early hours of the morning, breathing in the night air, warm and scented. Wherever we went we had fun. We were always laughing.

Henri and I had discussed the future during our holiday. War seemed inevitable although everyone was hoping it would not come to that. Nevertheless, I had agreed to give up my flat in Paris and come south. In the meantime I was going to England for a month as I had already reserved a room at Champneys, a health resort in Hertfordshire. The resort was fashionable at the time. For some reason, before I finally married in France, I wanted to spend some time in England.

I left Henri in Marseille and managed to get a seat in the Paris Express. It was crowded with soldiers who had already received their call-up papers, and with the civilians trying to return to their homes in the north or in England. Paris was in uproar. I cried when I said goodbye to my little flat, the first real home of my own. My concierge took me in her arms and wished me luck, and we both cried. She was going to stay with her sister in the country until such time as war was declared or otherwise. I never saw her again. She was killed in an air raid by our bombers.

I had a farewell dinner with Stephanie in a little restaurant near Pigalle. For once in our lives we had nothing to say to each other. She had found a little place of her own for the time being and was glad of the little bits and pieces I could give her from my flat in the rue Sainte-Anne.

The crossing from France over the Channel was ghastly and so was my arrival in London. I had booked a room at the Strand Palace Hotel for a few days, then I was supposed to be going off to Champneys. I found the hotel full of the most depressing European refugees and was sorry I hadn't bothered to find a more congenial place.

I had a very good friend in Cannes, Andrée Digard, whose daughter Micheline was a student in a convent in Weybridge in Surrey. In spite of the difference in our ages, Micheline and I were close friends and have remained so all these years. Micheline was to spend Sunday with me in London, so I caught an early train, picked her up at her convent and we made our way back to London. At Waterloo station we noticed abnormal activity, people rushing all over the platform, troops everywhere, and women and children crying. It was 3 September 1939. War had been declared while we were on the train.

We were both absolutely stunned. Of course I had been half expecting a war but when it finally came it was a blow to me as it was to millions of others. I immediately cancelled the booking at the health resort, convinced that with such a war the starvation diet would come soon enough. In any case I hoped the money I saved would keep me in London until I had planned my immediate future. Poor Micheline was just a kid and she was afraid to be left behind in Weybridge, as she hated convent life. When I left her at Weybridge that night she was sobbing her heart out and begging me not to leave her behind in England.

I felt terribly lonely that night and found it hard to arrive at any solution. The next norning I went to a recruiting office and made enquiries about joining one of the forces. They were as disorganised as I was and suggested I work in a canteen. Needless to say I was not impressed. Quite suddenly I made up my mind to return to France and to hell with the consequences.

The next morning I received two messages relayed through semi-official circles from the British Vice-Consul in Cannes. The first one was from Henri, urging me to return to France where he would arrange to have our wedding brought forward.

The second one was from Andrée Digard, begging me to bring Micheline back with me. The wedding news was wonderful but unfortunately we were not able to leave immediately as the Mother Superior at the convent insisted on receiving a written authorisation from Madame Digard before she would allow me to take charge of Micheline.

Finally, after a long delay the authorisation arrived and Micheline was installed in my hotel, but then we had more problems. New travel restrictions were in force and we had to queue every day for a whole week at the French consulate before we received our permits. The crowds at the consulate were unbelievably disorderly; most of them were Italians trying to get back to their country. We concluded the French Government was very short of money as they made us pay a shilling for every form we filled in. Then more queues for the British exit permits. But the British were more generous than the French—the permits were gratis.

With all these delays and the extra expense of looking after Micheline my money had dwindled dangerously low. I was beginning to worry when out of the blue came money from France. Henri or Andrée or both had remembered us in London.

The day of our departure eventually arrived. The Channel ferry was blacked out, and England was stoically and methodically preparing for war, but as we approached Boulogne sur Mer the city was ablaze with lights. We looked at each other and roared with laughter and Micheline said, 'Voilà la France.'

After that, there was utter confusion: troops moving in all directions, crowded trains and absolute chaos. Somehow we managed to reach the south of France. Micheline went to her home in Cannes and I to marriage and my future life in Marseille.

I had left Picon with Henri when I went to England and as it was the first time we had been separated for such a long period he was overcome with joy to see me return. Henri and I planned to marry on 30 November and the wedding reception was to be held at the Hôtel du Louvre et Paix, where I would stay in the meantime.

I was advised that as soon as possible I should proceed to obtain permission to marry. I will never forget the papers I had to complete, the forms I had to sign and the oaths I had to take and above all the stupid, idiotic behaviour of some Marseille officials. I had a valid passport, I was a citizen of an allied country, I had a birth certificate and an identity card. Furthermore, I was marrying a well-known businessman who had been born in Marseille. A German national could not have been faced with more problems than I was.

The official in charge said I would have to have my birth certificate translated. When I returned with the translation duly legalised he informed me I would have to have an up-to-date birth certificate, even though the one I possessed was only three years old. I cabled Wellington, New Zealand, and when the certificate arrived and I presented it to the official I had seen the first time he said it would have to be translated. I ventured to point out that it was exactly the same as the first one except for the date of issue. He was adamant it had to be translated. This was all too much for me and as by this time I was seething with rage I said some very disagreeable things about his exalted office, adding a choice piece of advice as to what he should do with his papers! Back at the hotel I phoned Henri and said as far as I was concerned the wedding was off. Henri was by now quite used to my behaviour, and my sudden decisions, and what happened after that remains a secret between Henri and the Town Hall. All I know is that several hours later my papers, duly completed and legalised, were delivered to me at my hotel by a gendarme. It was not the last time Henri would make things easier for me, and I never asked how he managed it.

Now that the drama of the unfriendly Town Hall official was over I could settle down and think of the wedding reception. Marius the chef and I conferred together for hours on end. We must have changed the menu dozens of times before we could make our final decision. So many of the ingredients had to be ordered from the north of France, and after all there was a war on!

Once it had been confirmed that we could obtain some sole, I determined we should have one of Marius's specialities as our fish course. He used to take the backbone out of the fish, fill it with the most delicate mousseline made with the flesh of *oursins* (sea urchins), then deep fry the soles until they puffed up, light and airy like a soufflé. They would be accompanied by a rich, luscious sauce made with *oursins* amongst other ingredients. For the first meat course we decided to serve loin of a special lamb—*pré-salé*, which Marius ordered from Normandy. It has a unique flavour because the sheep graze on fields near salt water. The cutlets were kept in one piece and Marius and his assistants managed to build little spits which revolved under the lamb with the aid of batteries. The waiters came in carrying huge silver trays which they held up high for everyone to see. The lights were dimmed and it was a wonderful sight. Immediately, all the guests stood up and applauded.

Whole beef fillets were chosen for the main course, accompanied by the appropriate vegetables, just as the *pré-salé* had been. Here again Marius and his team worked for days preparing food that was not only delicious to eat but also a delight to see. Once more the course was served from big silver platters. The cooks had taken the crumbs out of sandwich loaves, crisped the shells and ingeniously had inserted lights powered from batteries in the hollows of each loaf. The light-bulbs were disguised and resembled a log-fire burning under the whole fillet. The lights were dimmed as the silver platters were displayed, but this time not only did the guests stand up and applaud, they stamped their feet and cheered.

The whole feast and Marius and his kitchen staff were the talk of Marseille for a long, long time and it was probably many a year before anything like it would be seen again. The guests cheered Marius for having served gourmet dishes but the spontaneous acclaim was also to thank him for having been able to improvise in so many ways.

I was not a Roman Catholic so we were married in the Town Hall at three in the afternoon and went straight back to the hotel to join our close friends, all steady imbibers like us. A wonderful surprise awaited me in the hall—three journalists from Paris. Without telling me, Henri had extended an invitation to our little Paris group. Those who could not accept had sent presents with love. Henri's thoughtfulness was very touching.

Henri's family, who rather disapproved of the marriage, and other conservative guests were invited for 6 p.m. and we had both instructed the barmen and waiters to lace their drinks with care. It proved to be a wise decision as soon, one by one, they forgot all about their inhibitions. Ineed, some of them remarked on the vintage of the champagne and the sweetness of the fresh orange juice, unaware that their respective drinks had been reinforced with Napoleon brandy or Grand Marnier. Henri and I were having such a wonderful time we refused to leave, and stayed on until the bitter end with the journalists, who, of course, were used to such unconventional behaviour.

My father-in-law, who was very careful with his money, was positively glowing with happiness as his daughter-in-law had organised such a magnificent reception which had not cost him a single cent. Henri and I left for Cannes the next day. We both agreed that, in more ways than one, it had been a very unusual wedding.

CHAPTER FOUR

We booked into the Martinez and on our subsequent trips to Cannes we stayed at this hotel, where we were always allotted a corner room facing the sea and the port, with the mountains in the distance. We could see everything happening on the Croisette and the lovely yachts sailing in and out of the bay. All of my married life with Henri was as beautifully organised. Money has never been important to me for itself, but Henri taught me how pleasant life can be if you have money and enjoy it. The weather was beautiful and it was hard to believe we were really at war. It was called the 'phony war' with good reason. Nothing seemed to be happening. As far as we could see Cannes consisted mainly of visitors who had been caught holidaying when war was declared, those who did not wish to return to their homes and others who were living by their wits.

We had dozens of friends who were business or professional people living in the south of France and although we used to watch the antics of the shady characters with great delight we kept very much to ourselves, at the same time enjoying the fantastic life to be seen going on around us.

I found it hard to settle down when we returned to Marseille. I had been keyed up for so long, with the declaration of war while I was in London, the trouble getting back to France, the drawn-out formalities at the Town Hall, the wedding reception, the brief honeymoon. Now I was a French housewife: such a contrast to the giddy life I had been leading. Furthermore, I missed Paris and my friends, and all our harmless activities. I contented myself by giving our maid the orders for the day, then racing into town where I would meet my girl-friends and gossip over an aperitif or two. Then I'd return home for an extended midday meal with Henri, and then back to town, where my friends and I would do the rounds of dress-makers, hairdressers and tea salons until it was time for us to meet our respective husbands. No woman could have been more useless or frivolous than I was during those winter months, although I did continue to take my cooking lessons.

I had met Pepe Caillat, the accepted master of the great chefs of Marseille, who had taken me in hand once he realised my keen interest in Provençal cooking. Amongst other things, he taught me to make a real bouillabaisse *à la Marseillaise*. My moment of glory came when months later my father-in-law asked me if I would make one for a luncheon party to which Maurice Chevalier had been invited. That delightful singer and entertainer could not believe that the bouillabaisse had been made by an Australian. Pepe had taught me well.

Except for the families whose menfolk had been called up or who were already in the battle zone, the war did not exist in Marseille. Outwardly it appeared to be business as usual, although shortages of food and other goods were becoming apparent and prices were too high for the average person on a low or fixed income. We dined in town every night. Sometimes the dinner would be a farewell to a friend leaving for the front. Henri's turn would be coming soon and I determined to find something useful to do during his absence.

France was ridiculously short of ambulances and drivers. I managed to catch Henri in a weak moment after he had consumed too many brandies, and made him promise to buy me a vehicle that could be converted into an ambulance. He tried to wriggle out of his promise later on but I kept him to his word.

Eventually he was called up and all the farewell parties were in swing. Frankly, there was a lot of false gaiety in the mad things we did during the phony war. Rumours were flying all over the countryside and we were all letting off steam because we were bewildered and unable to believe in the leaders any longer.

Since my return to Marseille I had been accumulating enough tinned foods to last us several years. Sacks of coffee, sugar and tea were in every available cupboard. We had enough cigarettes to stock a tobacconist's shop and the cellar held every imaginable aperitif and liquor as well as hundreds and hundreds of bottles of wine. I don't know whether I'd been intending to barricade myself in the apartment, living on our provisions until the end of the war, but it certainly did not turn out that way. Most of the provisions were passed over to people who had not had the foresight or the money to fill their cupboards. And as the war and occupation continued our home always seemed to be full of visitors at meal times. Henri was hospitable by nature and I cannot bear to think people are going hungry, so between the two of us we had very little to eat ourselves by the end of 1942.

Although Henri had received his call-up papers, his class was deferred until sometime in 1940. We could, therefore, plan our first Christmas, which we were going to spend high up in the mountains in the Alpes Maritimes at the home of the friend who had been my witness when I married. He was a doctor of medicine and the mayor of the little village where he practised and lived, and all our mutual friends were coming from Cannes to join in the festivities.

This doctor was loved by his patients, many of whom lived higher up the mountainside. If they could not pay his fees they would give him food instead. That Christmas we feasted on a variety of game and delicious baby lambs, a speciality of the area. He was also a member of the municipal government in Nice and in later years he helped me in dozens of ways when I became a courier for the Resistance.

All the guests shared the same views so we could talk freely about the war and the Germans, but everyone agreed there was not much we could do at this stage. So why not enjoy ourselves?

Several weeks later Henri was notified to collect his uniform as his departure date was drawing nearer. By now everyone with any common sense at all knew that France was short of planes, tanks and armaments, and so on, but we had not thought of uniforms until we saw Henri return from the barracks with the issue of clothing he had been given. Although it was in the middle of winter he had been issued with a pair of white summer breeches as worn by the Legion. The boots were too small but the clerk had said he should try to change them with someone else. No socks, but puttees from World War I. No shirt, tie or jacket but a greatcoat which was twice his size, and a képi.

We phoned our close friends and invited them for dinner, and after coffee Henri dressed in his new uniform. We laughed so much the next-door neighbours rang, not to complain but to know why we were so merry. We invited them in and Henri paraded once more. Then he wore my gas-mask and my best fur-lined gloves. It was an hilarious dinner party. Henri took his greatcoat to a tailor, who unpicked it and made it fit him perfectly, and then ordered everything else he needed. He had the money to do so, but hundreds of other men were not so fortunate. Although we'd enjoyed the farce we were disgusted to see how casual and inefficient the military establishments could be.

The phony war ended in March 1940, shortly after Henri had received his marching orders and left for an unknown destination. The Germans invaded the Low Countries and before long the British were driven out of Europe. The French army collapsed, demoralised.

I joined a small voluntary ambulance unit, driving the ambulance Henri had provided. As we drove to the north of France we met Belgian refugees already streaming down the highways on their way south. The impression I had formed of the Germans years before in Vienna and Berlin did not improve as I watched their aircraft strafing civilians—old women, old men, children, or anything that moved. It was a horrifying sight, especially the bodies of the children. Our unit was inadequate—there were so many refugees and so few of us; we couldn't help them all.

This chaotic situation went on for days and days. There were orders and then counter-orders; no one seemed to know what was going on, except that the Germans were approaching rapidly. We had a brief conference and decided to return to Marseille. But first we took as many people as we could and deposited them in Nimes. I stayed the night of June 13 in a tiny hotel, to be told the next day that Paris had fallen.

The French Prime Minister, Paul Reynaud, resigned on 16 June, and Marshal Pétain then took over the reins of the country and formed a ministry. Six days later the Armistice Convention was signed. It was intended to remain in force until the conclusion of a peace treaty. I cried for days. My feeling of despair was profound and millions of French people felt even more deeply. On 25 June the line of demarcation was established separating the Occupied Zone from the so-called Free Zone, governed from Vichy. The demarcation remained in force until the Germans occupied the entire country on 11 November 1942.

When at last Henri returned to Marseille, we gradually settled into our home and tried to take stock of the situation.

From time to time, since the end of World War II, countless efforts have been made by a variety of individuals and would-be experts to belittle the attitude of the French people both during the German invasion and the subsequent occupation of their country. France was shamefully ill-prepared for the war, but after the people's initial shock at its declaration, they were frankly unable to contemplate the possibility of defeat. After all, had not a succession of governments and politicians led them to believe the Maginot Line was invincible, and that their army was well-equipped, well-armed and well informed? How misinformed they had been!

During the phony war, all over France, people seemed determined to reassure each other that there was no real danger and that their magnificent army would stop the enemy from invading France. Just days before the defeat, General Gamelin assured the people that Germany was on the verge of collapse.

Although Denmark and Norway had been invaded by the Germans in April 1940, no one seemed prepared for the attack on Holland, Luxembourg and Belgium on 10 May. The Allied troops could not hold Hitler's Panzer divisions as they swooped further south, and the exodus began.

As far as the French people were concerned their *joie de vivre* had vanished overnight. They had Germans to the north, Mussolini to the east, the Atlantic ocean to the west, and in the south the formidable Pyrenees separating France from Spain.

When beautiful Paris had been declared an 'open city' by General Weygand and was soon to be under the German boot, few people could control their tears. The French faced a bleak furure. The long carefree days were over—now the sorrow would begin.

The British Expeditionary Force had got out of France from Dunkirk early in June. They withdrew the best way they could, and as quickly as they could. Rightly or wrongly, the

French felt let down. So did I. After the war, when all the facts were known, it had obviously been the only solution. Nevertheless, the departure of the BEF was of enormous value to the German propaganda machine as they began to stir up anti-British feelings amongst the French.

If the declaration of World War II had brought gloom to the people of France, the surrender and Armistice was a hundred times worse; they were literally stunned. When the great French hero of World War I, Pétain, was appointed Head of State by the Germans, many people were convinced he would be astute enough to save his country from further humiliation, but alas he proved to be little more than a puppet figurehead.

As French soldiers were being demobilised some of them were assured by their officers that Pétain could still save France. They were advised to join the Veterans' Legion and return to their homes and wait for the signal which would come from the saviour of France, Pétain. They waited in vain. Within a year the Veterans' Legion had been enveloped by an organisation which did not appear to flourish, so the Service d'ordre de la Légion was created. They swore to fight democracy, the Jews and supporters of de Gaulle's movement. They were 25,000 strong when in 1943 their organisation was dissolved and replaced by the dreaded Milice, a paramilitary force which arrested many of our Resistance workers.

On the other hand, over a million soldiers were prisoners-of-war and the Germans were more or less threatening to take reprisals against them if the civilians did not behave. To make matters worse, as the soldiers returned we were absolutely bewildered to hear their stories of mass betrayal within the army. Boxes of ammunition had been filled with stones, road signs and directions had been tampered with, French officers, or men appearing to be them, had issued orders that proved to be false. The stories went on and on, but even so, allowing for exaggeration, some of them had to be true.

It is history now that the people in both France and England had been betrayed or misinformed by their politicians and people in high places. In any event it is heartbreaking to know that millions of lives were lost because of the dishonesty of some influential officials and well-connected families who looked after their own interests and bank accounts to the detriment of their country and that long-suffering man in the street.

We began to receive garbled reports accusing the British of having attacked the French Fleet at Mers-el-Kebir. The Anglophobes were delighted; I was sceptical and could not bring myself to believe the rumours. Soon afterwards the wounded French sailors were disembarked at Marseille. I actually talked to some of them and found to my disgust that it had all been true. I have never been so ashamed and disillusioned by Britain as I was the day I saw the wounded French sailors on the wharf.

Whatever the reason, whether Britain was right or wrong, I could only remember that we had been allies just a short time ago. I knew how I felt and I could guess how the average French person was feeling. The German propaganda machine had a field day. Is it any wonder they made the most of Mers-el-Kebir? One thing is certain. It made the French people, already suspicious of involvement, think twice before they included themselves in subversive activities.

When a war is over and all the cards are put on the table and one can see the overall plan it is easier to understand past events—after all, we all know that we cannot make an omelette without breaking eggs. But my sympathies were, and always will be, with the average French men and women who were stumbling in the dark, not knowing which way to turn.

How can anybody criticise the French for not having raced out into the street in 1940 and shouted obscenities at the Germans? Most of us sat in our homes with trusted friends and tried to think of some way of impeding the enemy in the course of his occupation. Another important factor should not be overlooked. Whom does one trust? Families and friends could be on opposing sides, so it was wise to be patient and tread carefully. All this took time.

Living in an occupied country is not easy. From the time you get up in the morning until you go to bed at night, the feeling of apprehension is always there, however well hidden. Once you are in bed, will that fearful knock on the door disturb you?

It could never be said that Marseille was typical of any other city in France whether during peace, war or the Occupation.

It had always been a city full of graft, of big- and small-time crooks in league with too many city officials and members of parliament. There was a strong Italian community, and many of them appeared to be ardent supporters of Pétain and peace at any price, perhaps because it was an easy and less dangerous attitude to adopt at that time.

One night I was sitting at the bar in Basso's, talking to Albert the barman, who was an Italian, and waiting for my friends to arrive. Several of these admirers of the Maréchal were holding forth singing his praises and sneering at the treachery of the British. Albert, who did not agree with their views, remained silent.

Suddenly we heard the noise of bombs—but who could be bombing Marseille? The war was almost over for us. We trooped over to the window and looked towards the skyline. Sure enough we were being bombed. By the Italians.

I have never seen a bar empty so quickly. One woman ran out screaming at her husband, who had left her behind. She in turn left her baby, who had been put in the care of the cloakroom attendant. Albert, and the baby and I were the only ones left until my friends arrived. Whereupon we all decided that Italians should stick to singing and not attempt to discuss politics.

We waited until closing time and as the mother had not returned for the child I took him home, returning him to Basso's the following morning. His parents never thanked me for my kindness, which we thought extraordinary.

There were two good things about that air raid: the Italian bomb aimers missed the main street, dropping their bombs on the old city where most of the Italians lived, and the Italians were all noticeably subdued after that night.

We heard about someone called de Gaulle in London, but in Marseille it was hard to get the news in those early days after the Armistice. However, it was not long before the saviour of France, Pétain, told us that an army officer had defected to England and that he would be duly punished when the war was over between Germany and England. Pétain, presumably, took the defeat of England as a matter of course.

Actually, as the months went by, Pétain was always good for a laugh as long as his fervent supporters were not within earshot. Most of us were sick of 'Daddy' and his portraits, his banners and his preachings of morality and virtue. Personally, I thought he was becoming a real pain in the neck. I was fortunate in one way. Although I was French by marriage all my friends knew I was a loyal British subject. From the beginning of the war I had refused to fraternise with any admirers of the enemy. Therefore, I could face the Occupation surrounded by friends and tradespeople who shared my opinions and faith. With me, they need not be suspicious and could say exactly what they thought.

Furthermore, in spite of my high spirits and gaiety I would always be discreet and keep a secret. As a matter of fact once I had promised to keep one, wild horses wouldn't change my mind. Unfortunately, if the other person did not do the same, I would be accused of being dumb, naive, or just plain untruthful. I once promised a girlfriend I wouldn't tell her husband I'd seen her that afternoon. Without warning me she used me as an alibi. It took us ages to live that story down.

During the war and Occupation I learned many things about my friends and tradespeople that I never revealed, and my discretion paid dividends.

Consequently, when I needed extra food, items of clothing, false papers or ration coupons, a source would always be available to me, though on the understanding that I kept these transactions to myself. Even when I got black-market food, I wouldn't tell my best friends which tradesman had supplied me. But I'd share the food itself.

My doctor friend had obtained an identity card for me which I used when I travelled. It was authentic in every way except for the place of birth, which was stated as being in Nice. I was now authentically French.

Not long after the Armistice we met an interesting French Army officer who was staying at the Hôtel Louvre, and we soon discovered he was already involved in some resistance work concerning the army. He had been intending to join General de Gaulle in London but his colleagues had begged him to stay in France as an organiser. His name was Commander Busch; his later codename was Xavier.

When he discovered we were going to Cannes one weekend he asked us if we would take an envelope for him which would be picked up at our hotel. We were only to happy to oblige. We continued to help him in this way whenever it could be arranged. Sometimes it would be papers, sometimes a suit case with a radio transmitter. Through him we learned that there were already people trying to organise resistance groups. This was heartening news just at a time when we needed cheering up.

CHAPTER FIVE

The Hôtel du Louvre et Paix almost became our second home — we knew all the staff from the manager down to the lowest paid kitchen boy—and they knew us. We would meet there almost every night for the aperitif. The front foyer was often full of German officers in mufti, so I preferred to use the back entrance which led into the little bar; not elegant enough for the 'Fridolin', as we called the Germans. In any case if they did venture into the bar, Antoine, the Corsican barman, would take their orders but serve them at one of the tables in the foyer.

I always sat on the corner of the bar facing the hall where I had an excellent view of the entrance, and Antoine and I would exchange rude remarks about the Boches. On this particular evening I found my usual stool was occupied by a blond stranger whom neither Antoine nor I knew. To my surprise he was reading an English book. Naturally, I went to the other side of the bar as I suspected he could be an *agent provocateur*, either German or in their employ—I couldn't believe an Englishman would be foolish enough to risk drawing attention to himself. He had only consumed one small beer although he had been there for some time, so I suggested Antoine should offer him a drink and see if he could get into conversation. The man accepted the drink, and returned to his book immediately.

Just then Henri arrived. Although he was a little hesitant he went over and talked to the man. After a few minutes he returned, saying the man claimed to be an Englishman from Newcastle-on-Tyne, and that furthermore, he was an officer interned on parole by the French at the Fort Saint-Jean. Antoine, who disliked most foreigners except the British, immediately offered a round of drinks. One drink led to another and by the time the evening had come to a close, I had promised the internees a radio, cigarettes and food. We arranged to meet the next norning at Basso's on the Vieux

45

Port, and our new friend was to bring two other internees to help carry the radio.

Waking up in the morning we had to admit that we didn't even know if we had been fraternising with our ex-allies or playing into the hands of the Boches. Nothing daunted, I went to Basso's a few minutes before my appointment, taking the cigarettes but leaving the radio behind. I confided in Albert the barman and related the events of the previous night, and gave him my English cigarettes for safe keeping.

Right on time we saw a small group of men outside the café—the Englishman and his friends. To our amusement one of them was sporting a big ginger moustache. He looked so ridiculously British I put my fears in the background and retrieved my cigarettes. After the introductions were made I took them to a place where I could obtain a few little luxuries for English tastes, and in the afternoon they collected the radio.

The man with the moustache was a British Army captain, Leslie Wilkins. We always called him Wilkie and it was the beginning of a lasting friendship. He was a little older than the others, and he and Henri got on well together. He had not been married long and whereas the younger men used to rag him about his wife, Henri was sympathetic and listened attentively whenever he mentioned how much he missed her.

The three of us became very friendly. Wilkie spoke excellent French and gradually we found we had a lot in common. Wilkie and I used to meet nearly every morning, go shopping and, after an aperitif on the Vieux Port, join Henri for lunch.

One day Wilkie mentioned how much he loved leg of lamb. He'd been so hungry on his long walk from the south of France to Marseille that he'd dreamed of eating a whole leg all by himself. I determined to surprise him.

Some time later my doctor friend gave us two legs of lamb. The meat was delicious as the lambs were running free on the most succulent mountain pastures. We invited our British friends to lunch. While Henri was carving one leg I placed the other one in front of Wilkie. His face was a picture. A young RAF pilot called Bob Hodges said he hoped Wilkie wasn't going to eat it all, but he did!

Forty years later the same Bob Hodges, by then Air Chief

Marshal Sir Lewis Hodges, introduced me to the Queen at a Buckingham Palace garden party.

It was enlightening to hear first-hand information about Dunkirk and other events that had happened in the north both before and after the fall of France. In the south we were already being filled with German and Vichy propaganda in the newspapers and on the radio. We became friendly with several of these internees and they were all given an open invitation to our home. Then we met a charming and good-looking Canadian who had been stranded in the south of France while on holiday. My young friend Micheline met him at our Christmas party in 1940. She fell in love with him and they were married when she turned eighteen.

Another Australian, Bruce Dowding from Melbourne, joined the organisation. We fell upon each other like a lost brother and sister, and Henri took us out to dinner to celebrate. Bruce had been studying in Paris, but couldn't get back there from his summer holidays in the south of France when the Germans occupied the capital. Bruce was proud of being Australian, but he'd acquired the polish of a sophisticated European. He was later betrayed by a member of the organisation who turned traitor, and his death was a particularly nasty one.

Henri and I began to make plans for Christmas, which we were going to celebrate in our home so that we could invite a few of the British officers. Six of our close friends in Cannes were coming over and we had all determined to enjoy ourselves. This may appear to have been an irresponsible attitude but my philosophy was 'Eat, drink and be merry, for tomorrow we may die'. Our Christmas dinner was a huge success. The menu was strictly French, except for the plum pudding, which is one British tradition I refused to eliminate even for France.

We were going to spend the New Year in the mountains in the Alpes Maritimes with our friend the doctor and passing through Cannes we delivered some papers for our French Army friend. Now we were involved in two separate subversive activities: supplying the Allied prisoners at the fort with a radio, cigarettes, and food; and smuggling papers for a French Resistance group.

Commander Busch's two colleagues from the French Resistance group were in trouble with the local police but after a quick phone call to our host we took them with us. They stayed with the doctor until, through him, they obtained new identity cards enabling them to leave the area. Several months later these two men were denounced to the police and I offered to take them to our own chalet in Nevache, where they remained safely hidden for several months.

Ever since the British had been interned in the Fort Saint-Jean most of them had been trying to find a way of escaping from France and returning to England. Others were organising an escape route. They were headed by Ian Garrow, a Scottish officer. Sometimes I acted as his courier, ferrying messages and later ferrying men. I used to wish I could meet someone who would give me a less boring task. I was at a stage when I longed to do something really constructive against our enemy, yet I was unable to find a good contact. I seemed to be on the edge of everything. I talked it over with Henri but he begged me to be patient. He was sure that when the majority of French people recovered from the initial shock of their defeat we would witness more reaction to the Vichy Government. I could see that he was right—after all, none of us knew who we could trust.

The latter part of the 1940–41 winter saw the departure of most of our British friends from the fort. After informing the French officials in charge of the Fort of their intention to revoke their word of honour not to escape, they disappeared from Marseille, hoping to regain England.

Very soon the remaining internees were transferred to Saint-Hippolyte-du-Fort, some distance from Marseille. Garrow had rescinded his parole and was hiding in Marseille. From there, he organised the escape route and contacts for other British officers. He was soon to be joined by a Belgian who had escaped from his country after its capitulation and joined the Royal Navy as a crew member of the Q. ship HMS *Fidelity*. Owing to a series of mishaps, including extremely rough seas, they were intercepted by a French Navy cutter and towed at gun point to the nearest port, where they were arrested. This Belgian masqueraded under the name of Patrick O'Leary. Eeventually he escaped and came to Marseille, where he was to work with Garrow. Meanwhile, I was still travelling regularly to Cannes and Toulon as a courier for Garrow's group. We smuggled men out of the country and back to England, with a series of contacts, safe houses, and a lot of trepidation as we showed our false papers to the authorities.

Life in the Côte d'Azur began to change for although it was in the so-called Free Zone, racist measures were being introduced. But as long as they were solely anti-Semitic, far too many people remained apathetic to the plight of the Jews. We were able to buy a very good radio set and now that we could receive 'Ici Londres' and hear authentic news broadcasts we did not feel so isolated. We had to be careful, as the man on the opposite side of our floor was a true-blue Vichy commissioner of police, so we always had our old radio switched to the Vichy news, and we always had to remember to switch the dial on the other radio to a French programme when the London news was finished.

Greece and Yugoslavia were both invaded by the Germans in April but several weeks later, just when the morale of the Anglophiles was at a standstill, 'Ici Londres' broadcast an exciting news flash. The magnificent German battleship *Bismark* had been sunk by the Royal Navy. There was much silent rejoicing. On 22 June German troops entered the Soviet Union. Most French people were amazed by this news. Russia is such a vast land and they had never forgotten Napoleon's defeat. On the other hand, Hitler's armoured divisions were advancing quickly and, to the surprise of everyone, the Red Army appeared to be retreating.

Unfortunately we had to endure many an argument between the left- and right-wing supporters. The Anglophiles remained silent. Secretly we hoped the invasion of the Soviet Union would give the British breathing space. After all, we told ourselves, Germany couldn't cope with a war on two fronts.

When I returned home from shopping one morning, Claire, our maid, greeted me with the news that Captain Garrow and another man were sitting in our little American bar. Furthermore, the stranger had kicked Picon out of the big leather armchair he loved to sleep on whenever I left him at home.

We kept three bottles on our bar—an Armagnac, a kirsch and a whisky. They were enormous bottles and sold only to important establishments for display purposes. We had obtained them from a barman, intending to open them on Victory Day and not before. When I went into the room I found Garrow sitting down writing and the other man in the leather armchair. I took an instant dislike to him. He looked, and was, very common, and did not bother to stand up when we were introduced. To my utter astonishment he had opened the huge bottle of whisky and was imbibing. His name, Paul Cole, did not mean a thing to me that day and I ordered him out of my home in no uncertain terms. My outburst obviously surprised Garrow. This was a side of me he had not witnessed before, and he left soon after Cole.

Cole continued to work for the network. He denounced many people and he stole from the helpers, all the time being a double agent. He was a thoroughly nasty piece of work, and disappeared as soon as he realised he was about to be exposed. His name was really Sergeant Harold Cole. At the beginning of the war while his unit was stationed in France he had absconded with the funds of the Sergeants' Mess. He had a criminal record in England before the war yet the authorities in London had seen fit to keep this information to themselves. He was also wanted in France for con-man activities before the war.

We didn't see Garrow for some time and once O'Leary came into the network we saw him less and less. By that time I realised they only came to see us when they needed the money, food or ration cards they could not obtain through their other friends and contacts. Henri was unfailingly generous with his money once I had made it clear I would help the escape network as much as I could.

Some time later I was told that several members of the organisation had been afraid I might become a security risk owing to my exuberant nature and British birth. Remembering Cole and the blockheads in London, I could afford to laugh. Their irresponsible assessment of the knowledge they had at their fingertips had allowed a petty thief to pursue his life of

50

deception in France to the detriment of men and women in the field, and with such dire consequences.

Nevertheless, I did not laugh later on when in September 1944 I was told of my husband Henri's arrest and death. O'Leary had been arrested and he sent a 'friendly messenger' to my home asking Henri to warn certain people. He was not a 'friendly messenger', and my poor husband was doomed. So much for their security.

In the summer of 1941 Henri collapsed at his factory and was rushed to hospital, where they diagnosed uraemia. I had never known him to be ill or even off colour, but he brushed aside my concern and said everything would be fine, especially as the doctor treating him was an old school pal he had known all his life.

In the meantime, our French Army friend the Commander had succeeded in forming a very good little organisation, comprising mostly friends he had known for a long time and whom he felt he could trust. He wished to be known as Xavier (not to be confused with the SOE agent of the same code-name). Although his organisation printed and distributed anti-German pamphlets, their main goal was to be in readiness for the day when General de Gaulle would call for their assistance in liberating France from the enemy. However, from experience, I knew that on numerous occasions they assisted Allied airmen and Jews who were evading the authorities.

I was delighted to be taken on as their courier, especially as I would be working mainly in Provence, an area which I knew well from pre-war days. I did not believe anyone who knew me would be unduly surprised to see me travelling, as I had friends all over Provence with whom I had never lost touch.

About the middle of 1941 Xavier gave me a packet to deliver in Grenoble. I was walking from the station and to my astonishment I ran into Stephanie and a good-looking Frenchman, whom she introduced as her husband Paul. Knowing Stephanie I did not enquire whether the liaison was legal or otherwise.

We were both in a hurry, but we had time for a quick ersatz

coffee in a bistro where we exchanged news. Apparently Stephanie and Paul were trying to escape to Switzerland as the Germans were looking for Paul. If they couldn't do that, they were going to return to Paris where they'd just heard of a doctor who helped people escape from France. That was the last I ever saw of either of them.

When Henri came home from hospital we went to our chalet at Nevache in the Alps for a little holiday. It stood high on a hill outside the village itself; it was always such a peaceful place, except when British planes flew overhead on their way to bomb Turin.

The transport services were practically nonexistent now in Marseille. The trams were always breaking down and it was not always easy to procure a taxi, so I bought a bicycle and learnt to ride it. From then on I went all over Marseille on my bicycle, dashing in and out of the traffic as if I'd been riding one all my life. Conditions were getting harder every day in Marseille, although I could not complain as I had plenty of money to buy food if it was available; but thousands of people were existing on a starvation diet. Pétain told us that France had lost the war because the people drank too much, so for three days a week alcohol could not be served in the bistros or cafés. On the other four days we could only be served drinks with a low percentage of alcohol. Then the Pétainists started denouncing the non-Pétainists and others denounced perfectly innocent people just to get even for past disagreements. It was sad to see human beings sinking so low, and with no compassion at all for their compatriots. I was lucky. When I travelled around the countryside I could always pop in and see old friends, and in Marseille I had plenty to keep me occupied.

For months Xavier and his team had been working hard trying to assemble an old printing machine, but just as they obtained the spare parts needed to put it in order, the local police raided the house he had been using. To their surprise, instead of finding the expected black-market goods they found the press, so it was back to square one for Xavier.

For a while he used to go to Henri's office to type his literature which someone copied for him, but the warehouse was situated in an over-populated area full of Italians and other curious people, and he was obliged to find a safer place.

Out of the blue an old army colleague of his, who was leaving France to join the Free French in England, offered him his little house on the Corniche road in Marseille. It was ideal for subversive work as it was isolated from the adjacent houses, but it was also on a busy road which made it easier for visitors to come and go. It was perfect for me as it was near a rock swimming-hole where I had been used to bathing for some time.

For months I collected his pamphlets, putting them in my shopping basket on the back of my bike and delivering them safely to various addresses. If we happened to meet Xavier in the Hôtel Louvre we would have a drink and sometimes dine together, but we never discussed his activities in front of anyone. As far as the hotel staff were concerned we were just casual acquaintances who had met in their bar.

By autumn 1941 the morale of the people had deteriorated noticeably. Most of them were filled with despair, and for many unfortunate ones a gloomy winter lay ahead. There was not enough fuel for domestic heating; food rations were not being honoured on time and frequently not at all; clothes and shoes were almost impossible to buy with coupons and were too expensive on the black market for the majority of people.

With Germany fighting in Russia, and the United States of America declaring war on Japan and the Axis Powers after Pearl Harbor, new hope came to the French. Even some of the pessimistic ones admitted that there could be a chance. Understandably, it is hard to remain optimistic on an empty stomach. People tried to cheer themselves up by saying it could not get worse. They were wrong. It did get worse. 1942 turned out to be long, hard and bitter.

When we next saw O'Leary he informed us that Garrow had been arrested. He was to serve three months' solitary confinement in Fort Saint-Nicolas in Marseille, after which he would be sent to the Mauzac concentration camp in the Dordogne for ten years. We were also advised to sever our link with Garrow's organisation temporarily, his place having been taken by O'Leary.

CHAPTER SIX

We were having our midday meal one day when Xavier appeared at our front door. We guessed it was urgent. His two right-hand men were in serious trouble. Could we help? The three of us put our heads together and it was decided I would take them to our chalet in Nevache. This way I could kill two birds with one stone.

I wanted to see the farmer who kept an eye on our chalet and ask him to fatten up a pig which we two would share. This was a normal custom in France but first of all I had to find a suitable piglet. Also I had to buy a little bit of land so that he could grow the potatoes needed to fatten the pig.

Next morning, I caught the train to Nice and in the afternoon our contact gave me two sets of papers, not only identity cards but every other paper the police would demand. We encountered no trouble when we left Marseille. The men showed the identity cards at the station and during the journey in the train. We separated when we reached Nevache. I went directly to the chalet while the others circled the village in a round-about way before joining me.

I found a little piglet in Briançon and after a very underhand sale it was delivered to the farmer in the dead of night. A block of land was available for sale and all I had to do now was to wait for the pig to grow up and become nice and fat. Leaving my guests with a long list of do's and don'ts I returned to Marseille feeling very pleased with my purchases, having arranged to return during the summer months with a family I had met in Marseille, the Ficetoles.

When France had still been fighting, it was customary for people to adopt a *filleul de guerre* if their circumstances permitted. Henri agreed with my proposal that I should have a *filleul*, a poor soldier to send food parcels to, but stipulated that he would be the one to select a worthy case. He sent me the names of three of his fellow privates. I chose the one from Marseille. And so the Ficetole family came into our life.

54

(Above) *Nancy in 1928, aged 16*

(Right) *Aged 19 in 1931*

(Above) *At Grand St Bernard Pass in 1935*

(Right) *A glamour portrait taken during Nancy's Paris years*

*Andrée Digard
and Nancy in 1942.*

(From left) *Lieutenant Finch (?), Ian Garrow, Paddy Treacy
and Leslie Wilkins in Marseille, winter 1940.*

Micheline Digard and her future husband Tom Kenny.

Ficetole had been a tram conductor in Marseille before the war; he was married with two young daughters. During the war he had been called up as a soldier, and soldiers were notoriously underpaid in France. Every week I religiously sent him food parcels which he always acknowledged until one day he wrote to tell me how guilty he felt eating all the goodies I sent him knowing his family was in need of food, and begging me to send the parcels to his wife instead. I called on the family immediately and could see that they were very under-nourished. Poor Madame Ficetole was trying to earn a little extra money by machining garments for the army. She received a pittance for all the hours she spent at the machine, sometimes until well after midnight. From then on she received a food parcel every week and so did Ficetole. When Ficetole returned from the front Henri helped him buy a horse and cart so he could start a little transport service. Horses were in vogue now that cars were restricted, so he did quite well. The horse was named Picon in my honour. Later, both Ficetole and the horse were to help me out of a tight spot.

In June 1942 the Germans demanded 350,000 French workers to help man their industries. They were to be taken peaceably or by force. Perhaps Laval, Pétain's vice-president, wanted to soften the blow; in any case the *relève* was introduced. This meant that for every three workers going to Germany one French prisoner-of-war would be repatriated. Only 50,000 young men responded to the call; thousands of others left their homes to live in small groups in woods and forests, where they eventually formed the anti-Nazi outlaw groups known as the Maquis.

The failure of the Dieppe raid by the Allies in the following August afforded the Germans and the Vichyites another golden opportunity to further lower the morale of the popu-lation. Their efficient propaganda service issued pamphlets and posters deploring this action by the British, whom they stated had sent the 5,000 Canadians to a certain death as they themselves were too cowardly to fight. However, as the year went by we had some exciting news to listen to on the radio concerning events in North Africa as the results in that campaign began to favour the Allies.

One morning I found a letter from Garrow in our mail-box; it had been posted from the prison at Fort Saint-Nicolas. He said he was starving, and begged for food. He'd completed three months of solitary confinement and was anxious to have news of the prison sentence which was due to follow. According to him, O'Leary had promised to engage a good lawyer to defend him. All this was news to me, and although I knew exactly where O'Leary's Marseille headquarters were, I certainly was not foolish enough to endanger that address. Besides, we were not supposed to be associating with one another.

Henri had seen the letter in the mail-box when he left in the morning and at lunchtime he tackled me about it. He forbade me to answer it. I suppose I should have listened, but I didn't. I slept on it before making my decision, and the following morning I told my husband I could not ignore a plea from a starving British subject in prison. As usual when he could see how serious I was, Henri said that I could count on him for anything I needed, although he disapproved of my involvement. His family were being compromised by my activities, but Henri was on my side.

In my reply to Garrow I made him understand that our mothers were sisters and therefore we were cousins. I took my letter to the Fort and asked to see the man in charge. A close girlfriend of mine came with me and waited outside in case they kept me! They would not let me see Garrow but said I could deliver food parcels which subsequently I did, three times a week.

Eventually, through sheer determination and perseverance, I succeeded in my request to see my 'cousin'. He looked absolutely ghastly. Goodness knows what he had looked like before he received the food. I remember he kept me waiting for ages. Sometime afterwards a cell-mate of his told me he had been trying desperately to tidy himself up before facing me. As for the mysterious lawyer, there was nothing I could do; but as luck would have it O'Leary came to our home round about midday when he knew Henri would be there. He needed money and stayed for a meal.

Over coffee I told him exactly what I thought of the Garrow affair. He defended himself by saying that a good lawyer, allegedly a member of the Resistance, had been engaged through a third party to reopen the case and defend Garrow. The organisation had also sent food parcels through the British official who remained in Marseille up until the time the Americans entered the war. Understandably, O'Leary could not approach the lawyer or the British official, who was more or less under the protection of the Americans, so I went in his place.

First of all I rang up the lawyer and made an appointment. He was indeed a well-known Marseillais. It was a stormy interview but he had to be careful of how he dealt with me because my husband was known to him. I was in my most aggressive mood and he was forced to admit that he had done absolutely nothing for Garrow.

This lawyer was a member of a certain French Resistance group. He is now an important figure in France so I would be foolish to refer to him by name. Nevertheless, I would dearly love to meet him in a lonely spot one dark night.

From there I went to see the British Official. I was so cross at the time I would have approached a lion in his cage. The second interview was just as unsatisfactory as the first one. The food parcels had been left to rot, along with similar parcels for other people, in a huge cupboard in the entrance hall. Yet all this man had to do was to contact the Red Cross, who would have completed the formalities. Years after the war, when I was with my second husband, John Forward, then stationed in Malta, we were invited to lunch at Government House. I sat between the Governor, Sir Robert Laycock, and the envoy extraordinary, the Minister Plenipotentiary to the Vatican, who asked me if I had ever come across this particular British official in Marseille. My reply made him slap his hands on his knees and roar with laughter. We were both of the same opinion. I now had three men on my black list— Hitler, a French lawyer and a British official.

The entrance bell rang one day. I ducked behind a door and peered through a crack while Claire opened the front door. She didn't know the Frenchman there, neither did I. That was exactly the way we all lived in those days—always with those feelings of apprehension at the arrival of an unknown or unexpected visitor. He obviously knew Claire was on her guard when he asked to see me, as he immediately said he came from Garrow.

When I greeted him in the hall he took me in his arms and gave me a kiss from Garrow and one from himself, explaining they had shared my food parcels and the whisky I used to put in a bottle of cough mixture.

His name was Frank Arnal and we became staunch friends. He had appealed against his prison sentence, and had been acquitted, and he was sure that, in the hands of a good lawyer, Garrow would also have a good chance. Frank then told me that if the appeal failed he would give me a few details of a prison guard at Mauzac who was open to bribery.

In the meantime I went ahead with the holiday plans and we were soon on our way to the mountains, Madame Ficetole, her two daughters, a girlfriend of mine and last but not least, Picon. It was a long, dreary journey. The train was filthy and the engine kept breaking down, but at last we reached Briançon just in time to catch the one and only bus which was to take us to our destination. As expected, my two previous guests had departed. They had managed to hide there for a long time without being discovered and they had left the chalet in perfect order. And the farmer had good news. The potatoes were thriving and the piglet was growing bigger and bigger and fatter and fatter.

Towards the end of our holiday I got the shock of my life. Three Frenchmen appeared at the chalet. They had come from Nice via Briançon where they had taken the bus for Nevache, not realising that it was a dead-end route and that everybody knew everything going on in the village. They lived in Toulon but the Vichy police had traced them to their homes and, fortunately for them, they had been alerted at Nice by a mutual friend of ours.

I was not worried about the villagers in Nevache. The mayor was a distant cousin of the Fioccas, so was the one and only gendarme, and the priest liked me because I made donations to the church (which the Fioccas did not) and always sent him some tasty dish when I could as the poor man did not have much in the way of food.

However, I was worried about the authorities in Briançon. We all remained very much on the alert that night. From the first floor of the chalet we could see if any cars came up the mountains towards Nevache, but all was calm.

The young people in the village had been trying to get me to let them have a dance in the chalet, because dancing was strictly forbidden in those days. I had always refused because of the mess I thought they would make on the white wooden floors. Now I decided they could have their dances and when they left the rest of us would scrub the floors clean again. I calculated that with so many teenagers coming and going their parents would squash any rumours that might crop up. Our uninvited guests did not stay long but they enjoyed the unorthodox holiday, and the dancing, and some months later they reached North Africa. We left the chalet the day after they did and returned to Marseille.

Garrow lost his appeal. Henri and I, plus the girlfriend who used to wait for me outside the prison, went to the Gare Saint-Charles to see him being transferred from the prison truck on to the train with the other prisoners. They were all manacled together and dragging leg-chains. It was a miserable sight and the three of us found it hard to hold back our tears. We had seen many shocking and disturbing things since the beginning of the war, machine-gunned children included, yet these depressed-looking underfed prisoners, one of whom we'd known as a healthy man, affected us deeply. Everything was getting worse, and it was hard to keep our optimistic outlook.

I went to Toulon the next morning and saw Frank Arnal. Armed with more details about the prison guard in question, I confronted O'Leary. I felt I had him at a distinct disadvantage. His choice of a lawyer, or rather the advice he had accepted in this regard, had been a complete failure. He accepted my suggestion. I would do all the preliminary work and his organisation would take over the escape from the prison and France. It was useless to go to Mauzac until I heard from Garrow. We needed to know the precise whereabouts of the camp, the exact days and hours for visiting the inmates, plus the availability of accommodation for me in the immediate area.

The day before I was due to leave on one of my regular trips along the south coast on an errand for Xavier, he asked if I would mind taking a personal message to a friend of his who had just been released from prison. He added that it would not present a problem as his friend had a chemist shop in Toulon, and therefore I would appear to be a customer. I nearly fell over backwards when he gave me the name—Frank Arnal.

Some courier work was boring but I used to enjoy my coastal run. I took a train from Marseille to Toulon where I spent a few hours before taking another one to Cannes or Nice, staying two nights in either of these towns before returning home via Toulon. In Toulon, Henri had introduced me to a retired professional fisherman who ran a little bistro down by the port. If he ever had any goods for me, edible or otherwise, he would put them aside until I called in on my return. His bar was a hive of activity and nearly always full of interesting and amusing people. In Nice and Cannes I had plenty of friends where I could stay for a few days and catch up on all the local news and gossip.

When I walked into Frank's shop he assumed it was something to do with Garrow. He was speechless when I gave him the message from Xavier, then laughed and said how delighted he was to find I was involved with such a reliable and dedicated man. Frank and I were staunch friends from the time we met, but now we had an extra special bond.

Eventually I received a letter from Garrow. Mauzac was a Vichyiste concentration camp situated on the Dordogne River about twenty-four kilometres from the little town of Bergerac. From Marseille it was a long, tedious journey by train. I would take the Bordeaux express as far as Agen, then the Perigueux train to a little place that connected with the Sarlat–Bergerac line. Frank had not been given the name of the guard I wished to contact and he advised me to make myself as conspicuous as possible in the hope that he would make himself known.

I left Marseille on 11 November 1942, intending to stay in the area of the camp for the weekend, which meant I could visit Garrow on Saturday and Sunday. Henri had been able to reserve me a return seat on the Bordeaux train. Although he had not wanted me to be involved with this affair, once I had made my own decision he always did everything to make my task easier. Conflicting rumours were flying all over the city. Henri suggested I put my trip off until the following week but I had organised my accommodation and decided to risk it. By the time the train reached Toulouse I knew that the Germans had entered the Unoccupied Zone.

The camp was within walking distance of my lodgings. As I approached I could see groups of men standing talking to each other behind the barbed wire surrounding the enclosure. I had to walk right past them to get to the entrance and I could feel all the eyes following me. Suddenly they shouted out loud, and Garrow appeared. They had been on the lookout for me. Garrow had not heard any whispers about 'friendly' guards, so when the visiting hours were over I strolled around the area and on to the village, hoping for a contact which did not eventuate. I knew I had to be patient, however, and that it would be only a matter of time. I booked my room for the following week and made tracks for home.

When I took my seat in the train at Agen I was disagreeably surprised to find I was sitting beside a German officer in uniform. By the time I reached Marseille they were all over the place.

I continued my trips to Mauzac until one fine day a man on a bicycle passed me, at the same time throwing down a note wrapped around a stone. I was to meet him on the bridge at La Linde at midnight. I kept the appointment. He did not. I felt very disgruntled as I made my way back to my room in the middle of the night, especially as there had been an early curfew. I left as usual the following week for Mauzac. I was having a drink in the bistro in the village when a man came over and got into conversation. It was the guard I had been seeking. He wanted 500,000 francs and a guard's uniform. But he wanted 50,000 francs deposit and I only had 10,000 with me.

We arranged a convenient and discreet meeting place for that night and immediately I phoned Henri for the extra money. He telegraphed it urgently; I collected it at the post office and handed it over to the guard, promising the balance when I returned. The next day at the camp I was taken to the Commandant's office and he asked me why I had received a large sum of money from Marseille. Of course I guessed what had happened, but I pretended I had not received a large sum of money. He gave himself away by saying that the post office had informed him of the details of the transfer. He was a supercilious-looking man and I think he was, or had been, an army officer. Giving him a scornful look, I pointed out that whereas 40,000 francs was probably a large sum for a man on his salary, it was nothing for me. With a deadpan face I added that I needed the money for drinks at the bistro. He gave me a scathing look and ordered a guard to take me to the visitors' room.

Before I returned to Marseille I made an official complaint to the local post office with regard to their indiscretions and followed it up with a very strong letter to the main post office in the department of Dordogne. This is what an innocent Frenchwoman, wrongly accused, would have done, and I always managed to believe wholeheartedly in the part I was playing.

O'Leary was waiting for me on the platform as the train pulled into Toulouse. I just had time to give him details of the last two days and he decided to accompany me to Mauzac the following week. As bad luck would have it, the escape had to be temporarily postponed as the guards had been changed at the camp and a different type of uniform was required. Then to make matters worse, the French Fleet was scuttled in Toulon on 27 November. The Germans were furious and tightened up the regulations, which made travelling more dangerous. Altogether it was a depressing and frustrating time, a combination which sometimes leads to mistakes made through sheer impatience.

O'Leary procured the new uniform. The guard smuggled it into the camp and hid it in a lavatory. On 8 December Garrow put it on and marched out at the changing of the guard. A car was waiting for him nearby and he was whisked away to Toulouse. After recuperating and being prepared for the arduous trek over the Pyrenees he finally arrived safely back in England.

To assist in Garrow's escape, O'Leary had picked three men. One was his wireless operator, Tom Groome, who had recently arrived from London. Tom was tall and good-looking and completely bilingual. His mother was French and his father Australian.

Several weeks after Garrow's escape, Tom and his assistant, a young French girl, were arrested by the Gestapo as Tom was tapping out a message to London. They were both escorted to the second floor of the Gestapo Headquarters in Toulouse. Tom obviously decided that the risk of death was preferable to torture, so he careered across the room and jumped through the closed windows. He managed to run some distance and found a hiding place in a little passageway, but unfortunately a man who'd seen the escape denounced him and he was recaptured.

In the meantime his assistant showed great presence of mind during the commotion. She walked quietly out the front door of the Gestapo Headquarters and alerted the organisation.

Tom Groome's courage was an inspiration to all of us. I didn't see him again until he and O'Leary came back from Dachau in 1945. Tom has never told me any details of the treatment he received at the hands of the Germans, but I've read many gruesome reports, and can only too well imagine it.

As for me, after Garrow's escape I made sure I was seen all over Marseille by dozens of people for more than a week.

Some days later a gendarme called at our home to inform me that my cousin had escaped from Mauzac. First of all I expressed doubt, then joy, and after offering him a drink, which he accepted, I rang Henri to give him the good news. Once again I acted my part out to the full. If, as we suspected, the Gestapo tapped our telephone, what could be more natural than Madame Fiocca happily telling her husband that her cousin was on his way home?

It was with mixed feelings that I agreed to undertake a quick trip to Paris for Xavier. The papers I travelled on would be near perfect. Frank arranged for me to stay with a close friend of his, an industrial chemist, and Xavier organised a look-out on each side of the demarcation line to check that I passed the controls safely. But why was I going to Paris? What was my coverstory? I was not foolish enough to believe that the frivolous replies I gave the Vichy police in the Unoccupied Zone would deter the German police from interrogating me thoroughly if the occasion arose. I'd already heard that the Germans were looking for a mysterious woman they called 'The White Mouse', and I knew it was me.

So Henri organised a business trip to Toulon where we called in at Frank's busy chemist's shop. We had time to order most of his stock before we could catch him on his own. Xavier 'happened' to wander in to buy a tube of toothpaste and the four of us 'happened' to meet at our friendly fisherman's bistro for an aperitif. In peacetime this may appear to be a complicated travelling scheme, but in those days, especially in 1942, every angle, every detail, had to be carefully studied. One always had to have a feasible explanation ready for every single action in case the police were, or became, interested in any person with whom we were seen. For instance, Henri was on business in Toulon. I was on my way to Nice but had broken my journey to have lunch with him. We went to the chemist to buy some item I had forgotten. Xavier needed toothpaste and Frank went to have a drink.

After lunch, during which time we discussed our problems, I continued on to Nice where I had an appointment with our doctor friend from the Alps. As a doctor and the mayor of his village he had a special permit to travel by car. He came to my rescue and suggested a perfectly valid reason for my trip.

My false identity card would state I was French, born in Grasse (the perfume town) and single, and that official perfume business necessitated the journey. This would satisfy a routine inspection by the Vichy or German police but would be useless if I encountered any trouble. In the meantime we were going to try and reserve a room for me at a hotel in Paris for ten days—a red herring.

I was to start my journey at Grasse, where I supposedly lived, taking the precaution of keeping my bus ticket in my pocket. If I arrived in Paris without a mishap I would proceed to the apartment where I was expected and two days later return to the Midi in the same manner, but with an entirely different identity card. This precaution was in case the same inspectors might be controlling and notice I had only remained in Paris two days.

Back in Marseille I bamboozled my friends by saying I was going to the Alps to fetch some meat and game. I never failed to bring back food when I went on a trip. We gave some to close friends if there was enough, otherwise we invited them for a meal.

To protect Henri I wrote him a touching letter saying I could not bear life in Marseille any longer and I was leaving him. This was in case I got trapped in Paris. As it happened everything went according to plan. I took the bus from Grasse and caught the Paris express at Cannes. The only scare I had was when the Paris train pulled in to Marseille. The so-called King of Marseille, a well-known gangster, boarded the train. Fortunately he was in another *wagon-lit* and that was the first and last I saw of him. We were hours late arriving in Paris. The Resistance in the north were making train travel precarious.

I made my way to the address I had been given. No one answered the door when I rang. I had been pre-warned about a certain danger signal in the way the doormat was placed. I looked carefully; it was not there, so I rang the bell again. Still there was no answer. I rang again and knocked at the same time, whereupon the neighbour came out of the adjacent flat and said he would bang on the common wall. Sure enough, my host opened the door, greeted me and led me inside.

It was an old apartment with enormous rooms, high ceilings and wide windows, and bitterly cold. We went into the drawing-room which seemed to be in the centre of the apartment and there in the middle of the room, built on top of a beautiful Persian carpet, was a little wooden hut. I thought I would die laughing. They had everything inside except the kitchen sink. A radio, two sleeping-bags, two small armchairs, a storm lantern, candles, books, writing materials, a little kerosene stove with the coffee pot on top, glasses and *pousse-café*. This was where they spent the cold nights. They had central heating but no fuel. They slept in their hut—I slept in a huge bedroom which was freezing, but I was at least as safe as one could expect to be in Paris.

They were wonderful people who went out of their way to make me feel at home. As soon as I had concluded the business which had brought me to Paris my hostess and I walked around their *quartier*, looking like two housewives with our string bags. I did not like what I saw, as I had known a different Paris. It depressed me to see the German uniforms, the swastikas flying high over that beautiful city. Propaganda posters everywhere, the collaborators enjoying their life of luxury and special favours, the beautifully dressed women consorting with the enemy, but more depressing still was the look of resignation and quiet despair visible on so many faces.

The journey back to the Midi was uneventful. Henri, Xavier and Frank were all relieved to see me. Xavier said he would never forget the service I had rendered his organisation, and I am sure he meant it.

Christmas was not far away and Germans or no Germans I was determined to collect my half of the pig. I ordered a perfectly lovely ski outfit and off I went to our chalet, which was in the middle of snow country. Four young Frenchmen who were avoiding the Vichy police travelled with me. They had been ordered to Germany to work in a factory and were hoping to find a hiding place in the mountains. The train was very late arriving at Briançon, by now over-run with Germans and a few Italians. We just had enough time to catch our bus to Nevache. I went straight to the farmer's house in the village while the men went cautiously to the chalet, hiding in the woodshed until I arrived.

To my delight the pig weighed about 136 kilos. He had obviously enjoyed our home-grown potatoes. The farmer killed him and cut him in half. It was a bloody sight to witness but not nearly as bad as an experience I had the year before.

I had bought a little pig on the black market. I am sure the man said he would kill it for me, but he didn't. It was round about the time Henri mentioned quite wistfully he wished he could find me alone sometimes—there always seemed to be men in our house. The very next day when I was walking down the Canebière I was introduced to two English girls who had arrived in Marseille from an enforced residence in a little village, hoping to get a train to Portugal. They did not have a lot of money so I took them home for lunch. For once Henri wouldn't find me surrounded by men. I rang him up and told him not to be late home. I used to do this if we had anything special that would spoil if the gas supply broke down. He was home on the dot of twelve, expecting some delicious treat. Instead I took him into the bar and said, 'Look, girls for a change.' He never complained about the men after that. At least he didn't have to take them with him everywhere we went.

66

Soon after, having ordered a dead pig, I came home to find Claire in tears with a live pig tied up to the kitchen table. I phoned my butcher but he couldn't leave his shop as it was meat ration day. The pig was making a terrible noise and I was afraid the commissioner of police opposite would hear him and report me because, after all, this was illegal. I went down to the bar on the corner and the owner advised me to hit it on the head with a hammer, then slit its throat. As for me slitting pigs' throats, my education had been sadly neglected. I rang the poor butcher again and he gave me a few instructions.

Claire hit the pig on the head, but not hard enough. I slit its throat, but not deep enough. The pig careered around the kitchen screaming. What pig wouldn't? We were covered in blood. There was blood on the floor, the walls and even the ceiling. Finally I picked up the hammer, gave the pig a mighty wallop and knocked it out.

It was almost time for Henri to come home so I raced into the bathroom to shower and change my clothes, leaving Claire and the corpse in the kitchen with the door closed.

In came Henri, and he walked straight through to the kitchen once he discovered we had forgotten to fill the ice-bucket. I shouted out, 'Don't go in there.' He replied, 'Why not? Are there men or women in there this time?' I said, 'No, a dead pig.' He told me not to be so funny and opened the door. His face was a picture as he looked at the mess. Then he looked at me and said with mock sadness, 'Nannie, how is it that with all the women I could have married I chose you?'

Fortunately our butcher arrived when he had finished serving his customers. He cleaned up the mess and cut up the pig, and when it was all over Henri used to delight in recounting the story. One day he saw a notice outside the abattoirs—'Men Wanted'; he sent me a copy by special messenger, attaching a reference.

The pig in Nevache, however, which died at the hands of a professional, was cut up perfectly and laid to rest in a large suitcase.

I had intended taking the bus back to Briançon but the gendarme and the mayor warned me the Germans in Briançon had been making enquiries about a young woman who had taken the Nevache bus. Once more the search was on for 'The

White Mouse'. As I was the only non-local woman to have come to Nevache there was every chance I was the person they were interested in. Fortunately the villagers thought it was because of my black-market pig and they were determined it would not fall into the hands of the enemy. They were unaware of my male companions, or of anything to do with my double life.

The four men managed to disguise themselves to look like farmers going to market and caught the bus after it left the village. My suitcases, the pig in one of them, were hidden in the back of the bus and I borrowed some skis and joined the bus half way down the mountain, just pass the regular German checkpoint. The Germans coming up from the garrison inspected the bus as it passed but they continued up the mountain road when there was no sign of a female passenger. The five of us left the bus before arriving at Briançon and hired a *gazogène* taxi to take us to Veynes, where we boarded the Grenoble–Marseille express.

By the time I settled into my compartment I was exhausted but the thought of the suitcase full of pig up on the luggage rack cheered me up considerably. But not for long. The ticket inspector told me that he had heard there was a curfew in Marseille. Now Henri would not be able to meet me. And what could I do with the four men sitting in different compartments?

At Aix-en-Provence, the last station before Marseille, a youngish civilian joined me in my compartment. He kept eyeing me up and down and started talking about the weather. I suspected he was German although he spoke perfect French without a trace of a local dialect. By this time the curfew in Marseille had been confirmed and so had his nationality—he was German. When he admired my skiing outfit I decided to encourage him in a harmless flirtation. As we pulled into Marseille I accepted his invitation to meet again. The platform was swarming with all kinds of police, including the black-market specialists.

When I tried to pull the suitcase down from the rack he was a perfect gentleman and rushed to help me. It was so heavy he almost fell backwards. I took the smaller one and we started to walk towards the railway exit. The only trouble was he was listing heavily to one side. I begged him to carry it as if it was light, miming at the same time the way he should do so. As we reached the exit the police pounced on him, demanding to see his papers and the contents of the suitcase. He put his hand in his pocket and pulled out his special pass. He was a Gestapo officer. We made arrangements to meet in three days time. I do not know how long he waited.

Here I was on the Gare Saint-Charles with four 'wanted' Frenchmen and about 60 kilos of pig. Suddenly I remembered Ficetole's brother-in-law. He worked at the Hôtel Terminus, which had an entrance from the inside of the station. Luckily he was on duty and he took the five of us, plus the pig, into an empty bedroom, where we could stay until early morning and the lifting of the curfew. It had been reserved for a German arriving on the morning train. We stretched out under the bed and although sleep was impossible, we were sheltered and felt reasonably safe. I knew Henri would be alerted as to my whereabouts and, sure enough, he was waiting outside the station in the morning. A young waiter on night duty had been detailed to whisk us out of our room via the hotel kitchen. The four men travelled on to Toulon and their next contact, while the pig and I drove home in Henri's truck.

Naturally, all our friends in Marseille were anxious to have news of the pig and we arranged a terrific meal for the following Sunday. One of our guests was Marcel, a barman in a night-club. He was very anti-German and very helpful, behind the scenes, to the British and the Resistance. That night he was on duty at the club. Business was very quiet so he was chatting away with a German at the bar, and in the course of conversation happened to mention that he had eaten some excellent pork for lunch. When the German asked if it was black-market pig Marcel had to admit that it had not been purchased with ration cards. The German went on to say that he had carried a very heavy suitcase for an extremely charming French girl and that he felt sure that it had been full of black-market food. Jokingly he added that it might have been Marcel's pork.

At that very minute I walked into the bar, followed by my husband and our luncheon guests. I, of course, was ignorant of the conversation that had taken place. I pretended I didn't see the German and headed for a table far away from the bar. Marcel knew that I had let a German carry my suitcase so he shut up immediately and pretended not to know me. We left after a couple of drinks. We didn't want to get indigestion! We never found out what the German was doing in Marseille. He did not return to the night-club and I'm happy to say I never saw him again.

(Above) *Madame Sainson* (centre) *and her daughter with three Allied airmen whom she was helping to escape from France. Behind them is an Italian patrol.*

The Sainson children (left) *with the same airmen.*

Henri and Nancy Fiocca and Picon (below) *during their last holiday together in summer 1942.*

Nancy in British army uniform, that of the First Aid Nursing Yeomanry.

'Bazooka' (René Dusacq).   *Henri Tardivat.*

CHAPTER SEVEN

Christmas was over. As we saw the New Year in I wondered what 1943 would bring. After a busy year I knew that in future, with the Germans occupying the Free Zone, I would have to tread warily.

The dreaded Milice was formed. It comprised a small army of vicious Frenchmen dedicated to ferreting out the members of the Resistance and slaughtering them. They were armed, being an auxiliary of the German Army, and authorised to kill. They were arrogant, savagely cruel, treacherous and sadistic. They had absolutely no compassion for any of their compatriots who did not support their beliefs. They were hated intensely—far more than the Germans were. I have known Milicians who have been just as violent as the most savage Gestapo agent. Unfortunately, too many of these low creatures escaped justice at the end of the war.

The Germans were taking the occupation of Marseille seriously. They were determined to destroy the old quarter lying behind the Town Hall, which was situated on the Vieux Port. It was a large area consisting of old residential buildings and a never-ending maze of narrow streets and passageways. It was possible to wander around it but a stranger would have been foolish to venture any further. The residents were a mixed bunch. There were brothels, prostitutes, pimps, black-marketeers, gangsters, forgers, people hiding from the Vichy police, refugees and some honest citizens whose families had lived there for years.

The Germans and their stooges organised a high-powered operation. Thousands of police were transferred from other cities and the whole area was cordoned off, then armed teams entered and cleared the area, arresting anyone suspicious. If the residents who had been given notice to evacuate had not done so, it was just too bad. They proceeded to destroy the old town.

Whether or not it was my imagination, I thought our phone

71

made unusual noises. When I picked up the receiver I could hear a faint click. Claire caught a man going through our mail-box downstairs. A series of events took place until it became obvious that someone was interested in our apartment.

The proprietor of the café bar on the corner of our street had been a soldier in the First World War—he hated the Germans. He was also a 'letter-box' for a Resistance group. We were good pals and I used to call in every day when I returned from shopping and have a little gossip. This particular day he said he did not want to alarm me unnecessarily but he thought I had been followed when I had left that morning.

I had no desire to leave Henri, Picon and my home but on the other hand I was not anxious to become a guest of the Germans or even worse. It was decided I would leave for England via the Pyrenees, immediately.

When the war was over I learnt the truth. The Paris Gestapo was looking for the White Mouse, but they did not have my identity. The Marseille Gestapo and the Vichy police were watching me to see if I was involved in subversive work. But before the Marseille crowd would come out in the open they hoped to catch other people in the net. Had Paris and Marseille worked as a team and not as individual departments my story would have had a different ending.

I did not sleep at home any more. We knew all about the midnight arrests when people were half asleep. I packed all my best clothes in a big trunk which Ficetole and the horse took to Thomas Cook's in the Canebière after I had left Marseille. He labelled them: 'Nancy Wake, care of Thomas Cook, Madrid'. Unbelievably, they were waiting for me intact when I finally reached Madrid. Ficetole had cut out capital letters from newspapers. When pieced together they read 'LOVE FROM HENRI'. I found them in the bottom of the trunk. I had been wearing the same clothes for three months and could not wait to change into something fresh.

It was a traumatic farewell. Henri and I had to act as if nothing unusual was happening. We were very aware of the Vichy police commissioner opposite. So I just sauntered outside the front door and called out, 'Back soon.' Unfortunately Picon understood and was howling his head off. Once around the corner I cried until I reached the station.

O'Leary managed to join my train somewhere along the line and on arriving at Toulouse he took me to the Hôtel de Paris, a haven for Resistants. He probably could see I was very depressed and invited me to a black-market restaurant for dinner, which was unusual for him. I'm afraid I was not good company. Everything had happened so fast, but there was no going back.

The weather was shocking in the Pyrenees and surrounding countryside, and although I made three attempts to leave for Spain I was turned back each time because of the weather. The third time proved to be a disaster. I was returning to Toulouse from Perpignan when suddenly the train stopped just before the station and we were completely surrounded by armed police and *garde-mobile* who proceeded to bundle us on trucks standing by. I fled down a side street but got caught between some demonstrators and the police who threw me into a truck, along with others, and took me to the police station.

The Vichy police interrogated me. I had been travelling with my real identity card except that it stated I was born in Nice. I couldn't give them the address of the Hôtel de Paris and I was unable to tell them what I had been doing in Perpignan. So I pretended I had been with my husband on a business trip to Perpignan and that we had argued on the train and now I didn't know his whereabouts. They put me in a cell and pretended to ring Marseille. According to them, there was no one named Fiocca in Marseille.

That night they accused me of blowing up the cinema in Toulouse, which had been showing a film starring Tino Rossi. He was a Corsican singer who had an unsavoury reputation at that time as he was suspected of associating with the Corsican gangsters in Marseille. Probably some Resistance group was responsible for the bomb.

Next morning the police said I had been recognised as a prostitute from Lourdes. I denied this and got a slap on the face. After that the vice squad came in, dragged me into another room and one man picked up the phone and asked for a number in Lourdes. He gave my description, had a long conversation on the phone, then slammed the receiver down.

He told me I had been identified and I might as well confess I was a prostitute in Lourdes, and I had also been involved in the bombing episode. When yet another so-called vice squad inspector from Lourdes identified me I decided there was not much point in trying to get fair treatment as they were determined to make me a scapegoat. I had never been to Lourdes in my life.

I had an Irish pound note which they had not found. It had been given to me by Flight Lieutenant Paddy Treacy when he was in Marseille. It had been signed by dozens of airmen, and was my good luck keepsake. Paddy was an exuberant Irishman, and we had a lot of fun. Henri would say it was useless to try and curb Paddy's and my high spirits when we were together. Eventually Paddy got back to England, but he was shot down and killed on a later mission.

After twelve hours my captors in Toulouse allowed me to go to the toilet; while there I managed to eat it without any ill effect, although I have not become addicted to such a diet. I was dragged out from my cell after four days during which time I had not been given anything to eat or drink. They told me to sit on the floor in the corridor until the interrogator was ready for me.

I happened to look up and a few yards away O'Leary was standing between two policemen. I thought he had been arrested and when he smiled at me I was furious and ignored him. He disappeared, came back and smiled again. I felt like braining him. I had made up my story and, besides, I was in enough trouble without being connected with him. He said something to the police, came over to me and said, 'Smile, you fool, you are supposed to be my mistress.' I gave him a sickly, toothy grin, convinced as I did so that it was the end of me. Not long afterwards he returned with a covered plate of hot steaming food and whispered, 'Don't worry, Françoise sends her love.' I was too tired and cold to fathom the mystery. I just set about enjoying the delicious food.

Shortly afterwards I was escorted politely into the office of the commissioner. Up until then they had amused themselves by pushing or throwing me in whatever direction they wanted me to go. To my complete astonishment he lectured me for having lied to him and dismissed me into O'Leary's charge.

74

He now took my arm and walked with me to freedom. For once in my life I was speechless, but not for long.

When we were well away from the gaol, O'Leary related the story. When I had failed to return to the hotel, knowing that I had been unable to leave for Spain, they guessed there had been some catastrophe. Someone they knew had a brother-in-law at a police station. He made discreet enquiries, learnt of the raid on the train and traced me to police headquarters. From the beginning O'Leary said he was sure I would not involve any of the organisation and when after three days I had not compromised anyone he decided to try and rescue me.

One thing O'Leary didn't know about me, and which I'd almost forgotten myself, was my clash with authority at an early age. When I was seven a girl at school had told me a witty rhyme about a little bunny whose Mummy wiped his bummy. I'd thought it the funniest thing I'd ever heard, and the height of wit. I copied it down.

Naturally, my mother found it, and immediately marched me to school and demanded I be punished. I was dragged out in front of the class by the head teacher and given a lesson in humiliation. I was only seven. To my eternal shame I denounced the girl who'd given me the rhyme in the first place. I hated myself so much for giving her away that I vowed I'd never dob anyone in again. The whole episode made a tremendous impression.

To be able to rescue me in Toulouse, O'Leary was first of all assured by a well-informed source that Laval, Pétain's vice-president, was in Berlin. Masquerading as a member of the Milice, O'Leary requested an interview with the commissioner, thereafter appealing to him as one Frenchman to another. He explained that my husband had never left Marseille. I was his mistress and we had been travelling together. This was the kind of story that was not only acceptable in France, it was appreciated.

O'Leary then produced the fake papers he possessed claiming he was a member of the Milice, adding at the same time he was a close friend of Laval. Although the commissioner began to change his attitude at the mention of Laval, he was still not convinced and prepared to telephone Laval's office to verify the story, whereupon O'Leary pointed out the fact that Laval was in Berlin and he was sure his friend would be most annoyed if Madame Fiocca was inconvenienced any further. Once released, I exploded. I wanted to know why he had kept my identity card if I was innocent, and I was all for going back and claiming it. O'Leary talked me out of it and promised to make me a better one!

I went to stay with the Françoise who had sent me her love and that delicious meal. She was a wonderful person and I loved her dearly. She was very ugly. It was hard to tell her age as she did absolutely nothing to improve her looks. Actually I thought she looked very much like an old-fashioned German woman the way she dressed her hair in two plaits. I never told her this because she hated the Boche so much I thought she might have a stroke if she thought she resembled the enemy.

Françoise was a chain smoker. She was never without the bamboo holder and cigarette in her mouth. She used to drink black coffee all day long but managed to put the holder to the side of her mouth and drink at the same time. I don't know if she undressed at night because she always appeared in the morning looking exactly the same as she did the night before. Her only living relation, a nephew, was a POW in Germany. She adored him and used to spend days preparing food parcels to send to him. She would cook all day and solder the tins of food at night. She also adored her cat, Mifouf. I often heard her telling Mifouf what swines the Germans were. Without a doubt Francoise was one of the most fantastic personalities I have ever met and I was very sad when she died years after the war.

For several weeks I attempted to cross the Pyrenees. Every time I failed. The Germans and the Milice were causing havoc all over the country, taking particular interest in the Spanish border. There were so many arrests that most of the contacts and guides were in hiding. Nevertheless another attempt was going to be made in a couple of days and I was to be included in that group.

At this stage, however, Françoise announced that she was going to organise an escape from the prison at Castres, which was not far from Toulouse. This meant that our journey would be postponed so that the ten prisoners she hoped to rescue would be able to escape with us. A guard from the

76

prison had agreed to co-operate on condition he was assisted in escaping himself. Françoise knew a friendly chemist who mixed a tasteless but potent sleeping draught. The guard poured it into a bottle of wine which he gave as a present to the chief guard on duty. Wine being in such short supply, he drank it all and fell fast asleep. Having all the necessary keys, our accomplice took charge of the breakout, closing the main gate behind him. The plan was a masterpiece.

The ten men were soon smuggled into Françoise's flat. Except for the guard they were in a filthy state. For days I washed and scrubbed their clothes. They were so dirty a laundry would have been suspicious. Françoise would come back from her shopping expeditions and give us a rundown on the local gossip. Naturally Toulouse was a hive of activity— Milice, police, gendarmes and police cars with sirens screaming, chasing all over the place for the ten men, nine of whom were sitting in Françoise's flat in their birthday suits, wrapped in blankets or anything that would keep them warm, while I washed and scrubbed day after day. Those days with Françoise were hilarious. That was one of the reasons we got on so well. We never shunned hard work, however disagreeable, but we always had time for a laugh. It does not matter how serious a situation can be, so often there is a funny side. The days we spent with these men were no exception.

In the group of escapers there was one Canadian, one American and several Frenchmen, one of whom—Gaston Negre—had lived in Nimes. He had been arrested when he was caught red-handed assisting in the reception of an Allied parachute drop. I knew Gaston well and had been entertained lavishly by him in his home. He had taken the huge key of the prison gate and wanted to keep it as a souvenir but Françoise begged me to try and persuade him to give it up. It took some talking on my part but he agreed eventually and I threw it into the river. I hated to do so as it would have made a sensational showpiece after the war.

The Canadian had been in prison for some time and was well aware of the plans. The day before the escape the American arrived. The guard went to a lot of trouble to talk to him and invited him to come along with the others, whereupon the American said he did not want to escape. He was happy where he was. Nothing the guard said succeeded in making him change his mind. At the flat the American had us in fits of laughter as he related his side of the story. Before the war he had been in some kind of a racket in Chicago. Therefore he was wary of all policemen. He had been shot down in Germany and without any knowledge of German or French had made his way into France, only to be caught accidentally by the Vichy police on the day the Germans entered the Free Zone. He was imprisoned and several days later was asked by his cellmate if he would like to escape. His answer was affirmative and he handed the chap some money he had hidden on his person. The guards came and beat him up—it had been a trick. He was transferred to another Vichy prison and almost the same thing happened. This time he was put into solitary confinement. When he arrived at Castres there was no way he wanted to escape! It took the Canadian hours to convince him it was all above-board. He was an amusing man and kept us entertained with his stories of Chicago. He walked around the apartment, wrapped in his rug, laughing all the time about his twenty-four hours in Castres prison.

Eventually the clothes were clean enough, but they had to be dried—a long process without heating and in secret. Françoise and I used to play cards with the men until the early hours of the morning, drinking pints and pints of black coffee. The police activity in Toulouse appeared to have subsided and the guard left for his safe house, wherever that was. Gaston had already arranged to stay with a friend so we said goodbye to him. The rest of us were divided into two groups and we proceeded to make our separate ways to Perpignan. I was travelling with O'Leary, a French Resistance radio operator, a New Zealand airman and a Frenchman who had been in the police force.

As the journey seemed to be going so smoothly I settled down to smoke a cigarette. Suddenly a railway official threw the compartment door open and shouted that the Germans were going to check the train. Almost immediately the train started to slow down, although there was no station. O'Leary shouted to jump for it. I pulled my window down and jumped and as I did so I heard machine-gun fire. I heard him tell me to make for the vineyards and the top of the mountain. I could feel the bullets whizzing by and I ran harder than I've ever run, before or since. When I reached the top of the mountain I was out of breath and collapsed. The ex-policeman was the first to arrive; he was surprised to see I was already there, but there is nothing like a machine-gun being fired at your rear to make you get up speed. O'Leary had been trying to see if the other party had made it and he arrived a little later.

The policeman volunteered to look for the other group. The unfortunate man did not return. He was arrested and died of typhus in a concentration camp. He was in his twenties, and left a widow and child.

When I had recovered I found to my sorrow that I had dropped my handbag, either jumping through the window or afterwards running through the vineyards. Probably the Germans found it and gave the jewellery to their wives or girlfriends. But it was too dangerous to go back to try and find it. Nevertheless I felt like sobbing my heart out. I had been fond of my jewellery. Apart from their value every item recalled some sentimental occasion that Henri and I had enjoyed together. My engagement ring was a flawless three-carat solitaire diamond, and I'd had a diamond eternity ring, a diamond watch, a diamond brooch in the shape of a little wire-haired terrier, another like a spray of flowers with diamond and ruby-studded buds. There were gold bracelets and some dress rings. I missed them already.

But at least I was still alive.

We stayed for two nights in a deserted barn. It was freezing cold and we couldn't sleep although we huddled together to try and keep warm. Each man took his turn to watch for any sign of danger. On the third day we started to walk to Canet-Plage, which was near Perpignan and was where O'Leary had a safe house. We all looked so dirty that we could not take a train. The police always suspected travellers who were not clean and neatly dressed. Soon we had to rest during the daytime and walk through the night, as not only were we approaching farms and small villages, but it was too cold at night to remain stationary for any length of time. We were all starving. Passing a field one night I jumped over the wall, against O'Leary's advice, and pulled up the nearest plant. Fortunately it was a lettuce. I hurried to catch up to the others and although I offered to share my find, they refused. I was not so fussy; I ate it, dirt and all.

It took us five days and nights to reach Canet-Plage. By this time we had not eaten for eight days. We had slept in sheep-pens on the way and we all caught scabies. Treatment by a strange doctor was out of the question so I had to suffer the indignity of standing in a basin and being scrubbed all over with a hard domestic scrubbing-brush dipped in disinfectant. It was an agonising treatment, but cured the scabies.

We were in a disreputable state when we arrived at the safe house, and completely exhausted. After a short rest and an attempt to make ourselves look less conspicuous, we took the train to Toulouse and Françoise.

Personally I was convinced that someone close to the organisation was in league with the Germans, and Françoise was of the same opinion. At first O'Leary, whether it was by wishful thinking or otherwise, was disinclined to agree. But he was, after all, an astute person, who had the activities of his organisation at his fingertips, and before long he admitted our assumption could be correct. Although O'Leary was trustworthy and intelligent, he did not have the keen sense of humour of my French friends. During his conversation with Françoise concerning the mishaps we had been having, he seemed to be using the word *si* (if) continually. Irritated, I said '*Si, si, si. Si ma tante en avait, elle serait mon oncle.* [If my aunt had any she would be my uncle.]' Françoise roared with laughter, but O'Leary looked quite shocked.

I had discovered much earlier on that O'Leary, who was actually Belgian, did not appreciate the subtle innuendos of the French language as did my friends in the Midi. One day I had mentioned the fact that an evader had left our safe house for several hours and that his absence had caused a certain amount of unrest to all concerned. He informed me the offender was a Belgian prince—the Prince de Mérode—and he did not intend to reprimand him in any way. I never believed we should favour any of the men, either because of birth or rank—to me they were all equal. He was visibly horrified when I added that the prince was only saved from being a *merde* by the letter 'o'. O'Leary's seriousness may have been because he was worrying about facing up to Henri. Here

80

I was, wandering around the countryside, when I should have been thousands of kilometres away.

My departure having been decided upon, Françoise took my shoes to the cobbler and my costume to the cleaners while I washed my underclothes and wandered around in a sheet until they were dry. The next morning, 2 March 1943, at ten, O'Leary kept an appointment with a fairly new recruit who had been engaged by his lieutenant in Paris. The recruit had asked to meet that amusing girl from Marseille he'd heard so much about in Paris. Pat had no intention of taking me along, and in any case I had no clothes. As O'Leary sat down at the table the Gestapo arrived and he was arrested. The recruit from Paris was agent number 47 of the Gestapo. His name was Roger. He was French and was also known as the 'Légionnaire'. O'Leary went to Dachau.

Françoise and I were alerted soon after the arrest. We were both convinced that Roger was the informer although this was not confirmed until later. Now everything fell into place—the arrests in the north, the mishaps on the Spanish frontier, the train trip to Perpignan when we had luckily been saved by the railway employee who tipped us off that the Germans would search the train. It all added up.

The apartment had to be evacuated immediately. Françoise was taking her boarders to another town far away where they would lie low for the time being. Unfortunately I could not accompany her. My shoes had been retrieved but my costume was not ready and I could hardly travel in my underclothes, even though I had a top coat. Bernard Gohan arrived. He had been an Air France pilot before he joined our organisation. He wanted to make sure we had received the bad news, and offered to take me to the home of a pilot friend of his where he was sure I could stay the night. It was agreed that he would escort Francoise and her party to their destination, return the following day, retrieve my costume, then collect me, and we would go to Marseille to warn the other members. At the same time we would pick up some airmen we knew to be hiding in a flat at Marseille.

Bernard was sitting in the train when he remembered that the name and address of the pilot in whose home I was hiding was in his address book in the desk in his room. If the Gestapo got hold of it I would be in grave danger. I will be forever in his debt. He returned by the first available transport and collected me, and we made tracks for Marseille. Fortunately, although I had lost my handbag and its contents, I still had some money Henri had given me and which I'd stashed in my brassière. I hate to think what would have happened to us if we had been stranded without any money.

As we approached the railway station I received a terrible shock. Standing on the platform, straight in front of us, was one of the policemen who had pushed me around so unceremoniously weeks before. I turned to Bernard quickly and whispered a few words. We hugged each other and kissed and acted like two lovesick people. I was wearing dark sunglasses and noticed the policeman was looking at me curiously. I muttered to Bernard, and we stopped and kissed and sauntered on. My heart was in my mouth and afterwards Bernard said he had been scared stiff. However, the acting on our part seemed to work, and we had no further trouble as we made our way to Marseille.

We informed some of our people in Marseille of O'Leary's arrest, and taking two airmen with us we made our way to a Madame Sainson in Nice. Not only was she a good friend of mine, she was also a member of the escape-route organisation, and I'd taken delivery of many escapers at her home before delivering them myself to the next contact.

We discussed the latest disaster with her at length. The three of us decided that Bernard should return to Toulouse and evaluate the situation to establish whether there had been further arrests and whether members had been compromised. He was able to contact his pilot friend and found the Gestapo had not been to his home, nor had they been to Bernard's. He collected my costume—I had been travelling with only a blouse and underwear under my coat, which I had to clutch tightly whenever I sat down or walked. Together with the fact that I did not possess any identity card, this had put me in a dangerous position.

We now decided that we would make for Perpignan and trust to luck after that. By now we had one New Zealander and two Americans, one of whom proved to be a real menace later on. Bernard had decided to come to England with us.

I took the airmen to a large store in Nice where we had our photographs taken; it was an automatic machine, ideal for people on the run. Our source in Nice issued our identity cards and we went on our way. We had been with Madame Sainson for three weeks. She had been a wonderful hostess and had taken a delight in all the intrigues that had been going on in her home.

Bernard had been able to inform two Frenchwomen that we were going to try to cross the Pyrenees. One of them was the wife of a man who had been denounced to the Germans by Roger, and the other had been the assistant to O'Leary's radio operator, Tom Groome, who had also been arrested. We made contact with them but neither Bernard nor the two women knew where or how to contact the man who arranged the guides for our organisation, besides which we did not know the password. One woman was openly pessimistic about our chances of finding him, but she always tended to look on the gloomy side. I did not know his name but I had an inkling of where he lived because once O'Leary had left me on a corner with some evaders while he went to see the man.

For weeks now I had been subjected to more than my fair share of drama. I had been forced to flee from home, separated from my beloved husband and my darling Picon, made six fruitless journeys to the Pyrenees, been thrown into prison and kicked around, jumped out of a moving train, been fired at by a machine-gun, sprinted to the top of a mountain, lost my jewellery, walked for five nights, been starved for eight days, and infected with scabies. There was no way I was going to let the little matter of a password deter me at this stage of the game.

I confided only in Bernard. I told him of my plan and recommended that if I did not return at a specified time he should leave Perpignan the best way he could. I ambled around the town, looking in shop windows until I was sure no one was following me. Then I made my way to the street where the man lived. I studied the house which I thought was his, and made a snap decision. I crossed over the road, went up to the front door and knocked. A man opened it and immediately I said, 'I am Nancy Fiocca, you are in charge of our guides, I work for O'Leary, so do you, I want to go to Spain, I've had

83

enough trouble getting here so don't give me any crap.' All in the same breath. He laughed and invited me inside, saying he thought I deserved a drink. I agreed. After the war when I lived in Europe I used to see him often. He was a charming man and took a delight in joking about my unusual approach. Personally, I did not mind if everyone laughed at me, it had been successful. Although he survived the Occupation his attractive little wife was not so fortunate.

Arrangements were made for us to commence our long journey immediately. We walked for hours in the dark and then settled in a quiet spot to wait for the coal truck which was going to take us through the military zone. On each side of the frontier between France and Spain was a forbidden zone, twenty kilometres in France and fifty in Spain. All the local residents were required to hold a residential permit, which of course we did not possess.

In due course the lorry arrived. We were bundled into the back and completely covered with empty sacks and loose coal. The lorry was checked several times en route but fortunately the cargo was not, and we reached our destination safely although extremely grubby. It was a sunny day and we were grateful for the warmth of the sun as we lay in a secluded part of a wood waiting for sunset and our guides.

They arrived right on time, both Spanish—Jean, who was in charge of the expedition and Pilar, a good-looking young woman who was accompanied by a dear little mongrel terrier. We removed our shoes and put on our espadrilles, and were soon on our way. The guides always used the high peaks of the Pyrenees, harder for walking but safer from the Germans who used to patrol the lower routes with police dogs. We wore the rope-soled espadrilles because they were soft and silent to walk in.

A trip like this usually took about forty-eight hours. After marching for two hours there would be a rest period of ten minutes. The guides always insisted that everyone in each group remove the wet socks, put on dry ones—everyone had been warned that an extra pair of socks was needed—then change back into the wet socks when the march continued. Some of the men used to complain about the procedure, but it was to prevent frost-bite. In any case it did not matter who you were, in the Pyrenees the guide's word was law.

The American whom Bernard and I had picked up at Madame Sainson's complained bitterly about everything. He had moaned non-stop all the way from Nice. It must have been embarrassing for his compatriot, who was a pleasant young man. We had been walking about twenty-four hours when the unpleasant American refused to walk any farther. I had not done this trip with Jean before but he knew that it was not my first experience of the Pyrenees, and he more or less put me in charge of the group while he walked well ahead and Pilar brought up the rear. I walked beside the American and told him quietly that if he was not careful he might find himself falling over a cliff. That kept him silent for a couple of hours. But it was too good to last. He finally sat down and refused to budge. There were two solutions: leave him to freeze to death in the snow, or force him to continue. I whispered to Pilar and she went on ahead. I had lost all patience with this chap. After all, we were all suffering, but we were determined to carry on. I dragged him to his feet, he sat down again. This time I dragged him along by his hair until he begged me to stop. He stood up and told me that as soon as he reached the American Consul he was going to report me. I don't know if he did, but I heard no more of this objectionable fellow. Not that I was worried about any consul, not after all I had been through.

We were caught in a frightening blizzard. We could not stop and shelter because there was no shelter, so we carried on and at last we crossed our final mountain. Jean led us into a hut and lit a fire, and we dried our clothes. One river to cross and we would be out of German-controlled Europe. That night we crossed the river and left the forbidden zone of Spain behind us.

As was usual after a mountain crossing involving our organisation, Jean continued on to Barcelona to warn the British Consul of our arrival. Pilar took us to the farmhouse where we were expected. We were given a delicious meal, after which we slept for hours while our clothes were being dried. At dawn we were escorted into the fields, where our breakfast and lunch were served, keeping out of sight until nightfall when we returned to the farmhouse for our evening meal. The farmer and his wife were kind and did everything they could under the circumstances to make us comfortable.

Jean returned with good news. We were to be picked up by car the following morning. He seemed a little uneasy and suddenly advised us we should sleep in the barn rather than in the house. Immediately we trooped out and climbed into a haystack, except for Bernard and one of the French girls. Before we had left France we had eaten some black-market meat which must have been tainted, as we had all suffered from dysentery during our trek. I had almost recovered but Bernard had not, and when he asked me for my toilet roll I only gave him a few sheets as toilet paper was nearly as rare as gold dust in those days. He grumbled as he went on his way, assuring me that the 'man upstairs' would punish me for my stinginess. I laughed and snuggled into the hay.

We were just dropping off to sleep when we heard men shouting and women screaming in the farmhouse. Then silence followed by the tramping of feet coming into the barn. They were Spaniards, but I could not understand what they were saying. Suddenly, Pilar let out a blood-curdling yell, jumped out of the haystack over all the machinery in the barn and out of the window, followed closely by her little dog. The barn was full of carabineros. They tried to catch her but she had vanished into the darkness. They had been searching for contraband or food destined for sale on the black market and had stabbed her in the rear with a pitchfork. It was pointless to remain in the haystack so we came out, one by one, to the utter astonishment of the carabineros, who stood there gaping.

We were rounded up and marched to a little village called Besalu a few kilometres away. We sang rude songs in French and English, and made the task of our escorts as tough as possible. Some of us were filled with bravado as we were sure the British would come to our rescue soon. We would sit down suddenly in the middle of the road and when they threatened to shoot us we gave them raspberries. We would stop and have a little waltz or a tango, or play leapfrog. In short, we behaved like a bunch of lunatics, and I am sure they were relieved when we arrived at Besalu.

The gaol was on the top floor of an old dilapidated building. Our cell was only about two metres by three. It was already occupied and with our group that made seventeen prisoners including three women. There was a hole in the middle of the cell floor which was supposed to be a toilet. It was freezing cold and filthy, and stank like a sewer. As I sat on the cold stone floor and contemplated, I thought of Bernard and how he would laugh while he was driven in luxury to Barcelona next morning. Perhaps he'd been right after all about the man upstairs.

We were locked up for three days with nothing to eat or drink. Jean explained that as they were celebrating an important religious festival in Spain it was unlikely the British would succeed in contacting us, as all government officials would be on holiday.

On the third afternoon I was taken downstairs and chained up, and they commenced interrogating me. All I would say was that I was Nancy Farmer and I was American. The Spaniards had been known to throw a female British subject into prison, where she remained for several months. I knew that Spain was short of wheat and flour and that the United States had either shipped, or was in the process of shipping, a large quantity of wheat to Spain. In view of this I hoped the Spaniards would hesitate before throwing me into some dungeon. I also hoped that in the meantime the British would be looking for me and guess my reasons for changing my surname and nationality.

A little later on they introduced me to a local tailor who had lived in Brooklyn for many years. He was to be my interpreter but I refused to elaborate on my story. However, I did tell him 'in strict confidence' that when the American authorities did trace me I was going to complain about the bad treatment I had received while in captivity. He betrayed my confidence, as I knew he would, and soon after I was offered something to eat and drink. I would only accept their hospitality if they unchained me and brought down the rest of the group to join me. We were all offered a whisky. Unfortunately we drank two bottles between us. It was labelled 'Pure Scotch Whisky Made in Spain'. We returned to our cell and were all sick, one after the other, in the hole in the floor. It was a pity because the food they cooked for us was excellent.

I was very lucky. They came and fetched me in the middle

of the night and installed me in a hotel; in a lovely, big, warm, soft bed. They took the precaution of placing two guards outside the bedroom door. It was most unnecessary as I had no intention of escaping. In the morning I was able to have a quick word with Jean. We were being sent by bus to Gerona. He was very worried as he was wanted for murder by Franco's government and once inside an important gaol, with an administrative wing, he would be doomed. He needed our help badly.

He was going to try to enter the bus first and take his seat. All I had to do was sit in front of him with one of our group and we were not under any circumstances to look around if we heard a noise behind us. All went well. Jean took a window seat. A Belgian priest sat beside him. We sat in front and when we were all seated each couple was chained together by the wrists. The guards sat at the back and front of the bus. Now and again the one in front would look behind to check. I could hear Jean fiddling with his chains. It was hard not to look back to see how he was progressing.

The guards on the back seat were busy chatting amongst themselves. Suddenly the one in front looked back to check on his charges and to his horror saw an empty seat. Jean had fled after managing to slip out of his chain and prise the window open. It was one of the funniest sights I have ever seen. The guards were all screaming and grabbing their rifles and trying to run after Jean. They did not have a chance. We could see Jean in the distance making for the hills. The guards fired a few shots and staggered around in the field in the cumbersome boots and their ridiculous-looking hats and came back to the bus looking sheepish. The rest of us continued to cheer and laugh all the way to Gerona. I saw Jean after the war. He got back safely to Perpignan and continued his work, but by another route. So did Pilar and her dog.

I appeared before the governor of the prison and was charged with illegal entry. He was a great big obnoxious-looking man. The trial was a farce from beginning to end. Mr Rapley, the British Vice-Consul, had warned me to be tactful, but when the governor enquired as to whether I had been well treated I said no and complained about the cell. I got an anxious look from Rapley so I immediately changed my tune and said that it had all been lovely. I was dismissed with a snort. It had cost the British Government £1,000 and a gold bracelet in bribes.

I will never forget the sheer joy of arriving, at long last, in Barcelona. I got on well with this particular British Consul-General. Once I had related the good and bad news from France and details of our subsequent escape, he told me to go out and enjoy myself. I did not need to be told twice. He invited me to a luncheon party a few days later and gave me some money so I could go and buy some respectable clothes, as by this time I looked an absolute wreck.

The airmen and Bernard had been taken in charge by the various officials responsible for their welfare and safe journey back to England. All I had to do was to make the most of the time I had to spend in Barcelona, waiting for the Spanish police to issue me with an identity card which would enable me to continue my journey. The consulate advised me to make enquiries every morning at the appropriate office. Every morning I went religiously to this office and enquired when my papers would be available. Every morning, without fail, I was told 'Mañana'.

I sent a postcard to Marcel, the barman in Marseille. He had worked for many years in Spain and frequently received correspondence from that country, so it was safe to send a prearranged message to tell Henri I had arrived in Spain.

Barcelona was a wonderful city for my little vacation as since I had left France I was sleeping badly, and now, no matter how late it was when I went to bed, I could not sleep a wink. So I would wander around Barcelona in the morning while everyone was at work, and enjoy the peace and carry on with the Spanish customs until the early hours. The food displays were mouth-watering and I spent a lot of time eating until I satisfied the cravings for certain foods.

I bought a pair of shoes, some stockings, two blouses and new underwear. The dresses and costumes were exceedingly expensive and not good value, so instead I looked at my own costume and decided I would have it cleaned, hoping the Consul-General would not notice it was my old one. The hotel manager was very helpful and sent it to his own cleaners while I spent the morning in bed.

During the war a British passenger liner, lying in the port

of Marseille, had been bombed and remained partly submerged for well over a year. The cargo included rolls and rolls of beautiful English suiting material, some of which Henri obtained from a friend whose firm carried out the salvaging. Although it had been under water all that time, once cleaned it was perfect except for a few watermarks. I had selected some of the navy blue and my tailor had made me the costume I had been wearing for the past few months. It came back from the cleaners looking brand new. Not only was the luncheon a success, I had lots of money to spare.

Then came the morning when my Spanish papers were waiting for me. I was to leave the following day for Madrid with the two Frenchwomen who had been included in our group when we left Perpignan. One of them was from Marseille. She was snobbish and considered herself a cut above anyone else. She was staying with Françoise while I was there and she consistently complained about all and sundry. She never attempted to help us when we had all the dirty clothes to scrub, and in the Pyrenees she had moaned so much that Jean had taken delight in letting her fall in some water. I disliked her intensely and my feelings were reciprocated.

I had met some Frenchmen I knew when I was collecting my identity papers. They were sailing for North Africa the following afternoon; I was leaving for Madrid on the night express a couple of hours after their departure. We decided to have a farewell luncheon party the following day. They had no money but I had the money I had saved on my shopping spree. It was a disastrous session. We were all a bit run down, not having fully recovered from the long march over the Pyrenees. We made the mistake of drinking too many glasses of Spanish absinth, which is very strong and which the Spaniards serve neat with a little ice.

We were all quite drunk. I managed to hail a taxi and deposited them at their ship, which was just about to pull up its gangway, and continued on to the station. As I was early I took the best window seat in our group's compartment and fell asleep; I probably snored into the bargain. The other two women arrived and sat as far away from me as possible. When I had slept for a few hours, I went to the toilet several times and disturbed them as I went to and fro. The fumes of the

90

absinth must have been nauseating for the two non-drinkers. As I was getting some scathing looks I decided to stand in the corridor and sample some fresh air.

I must have dropped off to sleep as I stood there with my left elbow on the window rail. The train stopped suddenly and I fell backwards on the glass doors between the carriages. They broke into thousands of pieces. The glass was obviously poor quality! All the guards scuttled around and the security police travelling on the train came to inspect me and the damage. The broken glass was picked up and the doors boarded up with cardboard, and naturally the train was delayed for some time.

We had not been able to find out the time of arrival in Madrid; the answer always given to this question was 'Wait and see'. The security guards checked our papers while they were there and took a great interest in mine, which stated I had entered their country illegally. The atmosphere in my compartment was by this time so icy that I preferred to talk to the police for a while. But in the course of our conversation they told me the time they expected to arrive in Madrid, which information I naturally could not pass on to my travelling companions as they pretended they did not know me.

When I guessed we were nearing Madrid I locked myself in a toilet, stripped, washed myself all over, cleaned my teeth, put on clean underclothes and my new Spanish silk blouse, put on my make-up, brushed my hair and sprayed myself with French perfume. I love purple orchids and I had been given one in Barcelona which luckily had survived the events of the previous day. I took it out of my handbag, brushed my costume, pinned it on my lapel and was ready for whatever the day would bring in Madrid.

We pulled into the station and the two women brushed by me. I suppose they wanted to be the first to see the British official who would be waiting for us. They looked absolutely dreadful. Haggard, ashen, grimy faces, dusty crumpled clothes, hair all askew, no sign of make-up. In a word, ghastly.

To my delight, there on the station, waving his hand, was a friend of mine, Jimmy Beaumont. He had just arrived from London and was on his way to the consulate in Barcelona, but

but had come to greet me. As I stepped down from the train he called out, 'Nanny darling. How do you do it? You just look as if you have stepped out of a band-box.' We kissed on the cheeks, then I turned and introducing my two scruffy travelling companions. If looks could have killed . . .!

Once my companions had been checked into the hotel where the British Embassy had reserved our rooms, Jimmy and I called at Thomas Cook's to find my two trunks waiting for me. He couldn't believe his eyes, as he had doubted they could arrive safely from Marseille. We returned to the hotel to have some refreshments and a chat until it was time for him to leave for Barcelona. Jimmy watched with great interest and amusement the proceedings as I registered at the desk. Whereas the other two had been left to fend for themselves, the reception made a great fuss of me. The assistant manager himself escorted me to an attractive room, with a balcony and view, adding, as he left, that I should call on him if anything was not to my satisfaction or liking.

The German officers sitting in the entrance hall and the lounge facing the elevator took a great deal of interest in me. They also took a great deal of interest in Jimmy. Why wouldn't they? After all, he had left London hurriedly the night before and was still carrying his furled umbrella and bowler hat, as all good Foreign Office officials do.

We both had a keen sense of fun so we sat next to the highest ranking German officer we could find, talking in English about mundane matters only but laughing and cracking jokes all the time. The last thing he said to me when he left was not to forget to let him know what Jimmy Langley would say when I arrived in England with two trunks full of clothes. As he pointed out, this was not the routine procedure for an escaping courier. I reminded him of the proverb, 'Nothing ventured, nothing gained'.

In Madrid I met dozens of Frenchmen on their way to England. We had all crossed the Pyrenees so we had much in common. I was never short of compatible escorts and we generally went around in a group. We explored the city and visited the art gallery, which was full of famous paintings; we also went to a bullfight, which none of us appreciated. Although we enjoyed ourselves to a certain extent I think they probably felt like I did; our journey to England was coming to an end and they wanted to get on with it.

It was not long before the two Frenchwomen and I received word we would be leaving for Gibraltar the next day. After another tiring journey the gates of Gibraltar were opened to let us in, and I was at long last back on British territory.

I stayed at the flat of Donald Darling in Gibraltar; he was the link between London and the O'Leary organisation in France. He knew perfectly well that it would be absolutely impossible to 'confine me to quarters' although I gathered that he would have liked the authority and the courage to do so. He contented himself by giving me a talk on security which went in one ear and out of the other. Not that I did not believe in security, but he was always so devious and long-winded. If he could say a hundred words instead of ten he would do so. In any case I had always been careful about security in the field.

However, he made one brilliant decision. He put me in the charge of his assistant, Ron Anderson. I think D.D. hoped a nice, quiet young man like Ron would act as a brake on my exuberant nature. It had the opposite effect. Ron brightened up considerably. I liked him immediately. He was kind to me, always courteous, and we became great friends. He shared a flat with some other young men and I often spent the evening with them. During the daytime I used to wander up to the Rock Hotel and have a few drinks by myself. There was not much to do in Gibraltar.

One day Ron told me I would be going to England in the next convoy but he thought I would be on an American ship—a *dry* ship. I nearly passed out at the thought of a long hazardous sea journey, perhaps with the enemy up above and down below, and nothing but orange juice and milk shakes to pass the dreary hours. Dear old Ron told me not to worry as he would see that I had a few bottles to hide in my luggage. Now to be able to buy one bottle of whisky or gin, one had to buy a case of sherry. There was so much sherry on the Rock I am surprised it didn't sink. We arranged that Ron and his flatmates would keep the sherry and I would take the spirits. Obviously Ron had never organised a transaction like this before, because it transpired that the entire order would have to be delivered to the ship. And it was a dry one.

At the last minute word came through that I would be sailing on a British ship with the two Frenchwomen. I don't remember where they had been all this time; they had probably asked to be put on the opposite side of the Rock! There being no necessity to take a supply of spirits with me, I asked Ron to cancel the order. For security reasons we were taken on board early, to find we were accommodated in a four-berth cabin. The list on the cabin door indicated the fourth person as being a nursing sister. Now although these two Frenchwomen, especially one, were not my greatest admirers, they preferred the devil they knew to the devil they did not. Therefore we took possession of the three berths over by the porthole and left the other one by the door. They took my advice and put their worldly possessions on top of their bunks.

The Governor and Commander-in-Chief of Gibraltar had been absent for a few days and he kindly came down to the ship to apologise for not having been able to see us beforehand and to wish us a safe passage to England. I was standing near the top of the gangway and just as he was leaving, up came a delivery man with six cases of sherry, three bottles of gin and three of whisky, and deposited them temporarily right in front of us. My name was marked in huge letters on each case. I thought I detected a twinkle in his eye as he wished me *bon voyage.* Our paths did not cross after Gibraltar, so I never heard his side of the story.

The cases had been taken to our cabin. I had a mental picture of the other two women seeing all that sherry in the cabin so I hurried to catch up with the steward. I caught him just in time, explained the situation and made him a present of all the cases except one. He was astonished but delighted with my gift, and promised to share it with the other stewards on 'A' deck. The rest of the sherry and the spirits having been hidden in my trunk, I gave a sigh of relief and raced back to the top deck to view the proceedings.

Being in a convoy is interesting. Masses of army officers were embarking. Apparently they had been in Malta and were on their way back to England. There were also dozens of Maltese women who were the wives of British soldiers, plus an assortment of civilians, all shapes and sizes and of all nationalities. A good-looking officer came up and introduced himself. I had seen him several times at the Rock Hotel but we had never spoken. The conversation was just becoming interesting when I heard someone shout 'Nancy'. I turned around and to my amazement I saw my young friend from Cannes, Micheline, the girl I'd removed from an English convent when war was declared there. She was holding in her arms her son Patrick, aged six months. Micheline had made the same terrible journey across the Pyrenees as I had, and she had carried Patrick. She raced away for a few minutes, leaving Patrick in my arms. I turned to the officer, intending to explain but he had disappeared.

We sailed at dusk. Everything was dark around us except for the distant lights of Spain. Returning to the cabin I found two very glum Frenchwomen. They told me the nursing sister had come in, positively frightening in her full regalia, and changed our bunks around. They never seemed to make any attempt to stand up for themselves and always left it to me to do the dirty work. We three were talking in French when the sister returned. I looked her straight in the eye and asked her to remove her possessions from the bunk she had taken, and also to replace everything else she had moved. She was of an overbearing nature which did not intimidate me one little bit. She enquired if I was French. I replied that I was not, I was an Australian. Without a word she took her luggage to the bunk by the door and replaced the clothes she had removed. She never spoke to us after that confrontation. We only met when we were all in the cabin. We were three to one and we always spoke French. So peace reigned.

The evening meal was late and the service was deplorable, but we put it down to the late departure and first-night staffing problems. A large whisky in the bar was threepence so I was as happy as a sand-boy. Even my companions asked if they could join me, so they must have been feeling very miserable. None of us could sleep that night; there seemed to be parties going on in every cabin except ours. Breakfast was worse than the evening meal had been and we decided it was going to be an awful voyage.

We were having a pre-lunch gin in the bar when the voice of the colonel in charge of passengers came over the loudspeaker. He said that the shocking behaviour of unknown passengers on 'A' deck the night before was an absolute disgrace and if it occurred again he would close the bar for the rest of the voyage. I am glad to say that was one party I missed.

It was not difficult to establish the truth. The bar stewards, not the passengers, had been partying. The stewards on 'A' deck had invited their fellow stewards to a sherry party. Other passengers besides myself had been informed they were to travel on a dry ship and they had also given away their sherry. When I told this story to my friends in London they looked crestfallen. There was a shortage of sherry in England.

It was fun to be with Micheline again and catch up on one another's news. Her experience of the Pyrenees had been traumatic, as I could well understand, because on top of everything else she had to feed her baby son. She was in a cabin in the bowels of the ship near the Maltese women, who were seasick from the time the ship left Gibraltar until it reached Scotland. The stewards cleaned the toilets once a day but as soon as they were cleaned the women would be sick again. The stench was nauseating.

Before long enemy submarines were sighted and the escorting destroyers would race around dropping their depth charges. Enemy planes flew overhead several times. I don't know if there was any action as our ship was in the middle of the convoy, protected by the escorting fleet.

The loudspeakers summoned us to boat drill every morning. Micheline did not attend, preferring to stay in the cabin with her baby. When the officer-in-charge noticed her absence he despatched a sailor to her cabin to request her attendance. I determined to watch the proceedings closely as I knew what Micheline thought about the boat drill as far as she was concerned. I was sure we would enjoy a little light relief. She arrived carrying Patrick in a little bath-tub which she deposited beside her. The officer was helpful and tied her up in her life-jacket, and proceeded to tell us exactly what we should do when the ship was torpedoed. Then Micheline piped up and said in her charming French accent, '*Bon*, now what I do with Patrick?' Everyone exploded with laughter. The poor chap was embarrassed. Then he said that Micheline should take Patrick in her arms and then put the life-jacket on. Of course, this was impossible. He was getting redder and redder in the face and our laughter was not making it easier for him. He informed the CO of the difficulties he was experiencing with Mrs Kenny. To save face the CO ordered her to take drill lessons with the rest of us but a seaman was detailed to look after Patrick. We were not torpedoed, which was fortunate, as I feel sure they would have encountered problems with young Micheline and the even younger Patrick.

The officers who had been stationed in Malta disappeared every morning between breakfast and lunch time. One morning I was wandering all over the ship trying to pass time. The bar would soon be open and I was trying to retrace my steps, but I got lost. I walked along several corridors but all the doors were locked. Eventually I found one that was not locked and in I walked, to find that around the corner all the officers were being lectured on security by their senior officer. I was surprised, but they were spellbound. I excused myself and made for the door opposite, which was locked. The senior officer let me out and enquired as to how I had entered that conference room. I pointed in the direction from where I had come. They had locked every door but the back one. They used to call me Olga Polouski, the beautiful spy, after that.

Ours was quite a large convoy and we had many submarine alarms but after about ten days we approached Scotland. The immigration officers came aboard. I had no passport but I had been assured in Gibraltar that I would be expected and allowed to land without any hindrance. When my turn came to be interviewed I found I was not on the list of expected arrivals and as I had no passport or identifying papers I was sent to the back of the queue. I tried another queue but the same thing happened. This was just about the last straw as far as I was concerned, but I was determined not to be beaten. All the civilians had disembarked except me and only the officers were left. I approached the one who had originally called me Olga Polouski and asked him to send two telegrams, one to Captain Ian G. Garrow care of the War Office and the other to Garrow's father, who was a professional man in Glasgow, informing them of my arrival. Thank goodness he kept his promise. Before long I was whisked off that ship and put into an empty train, having missed the boat one, and sent on my way to London. I was accompanied by a female conducting officer. No doubt she thought I was disagreeable. I was so angry about my treatment at Greenock I would not utter one word during the whole journey.

The train stopped at a junction before London and there on the station was Captain James Langley, who was on the staff of the Assistant Chief of the British Intelligence Service. I was carrying a small overnight bag and he obviously assumed that was the only luggage I possessed, because as soon as the customary greetings were made he directed me to his car. He was speechless when he saw the trunks, which would not fit into the boot of his car and had to be sent separately to London. We had met in Marseille but did not like each other. He did not appreciate irrepressible high spirits and I have never admired snobs. That day, however, he was charming to me and we chatted all the way to London, where he had reserved a room for me at the St James Hotel.

By the time I reached London I was in seventh heaven. Wilkie, one of the original group from Fort Saint-Jean in Marseille, was there with his wife Peggy. Ian Garrow took me to dinner at Qaglino's. Bob Hodges, a young pilot officer we had helped in Marseille, took me to lunch with his mother. It had taken me months to arrive but I had made it.

PART THREE

CHAPTER EIGHT

After the excitement of arriving in London had subsided it took me several weeks to settle down. I suppose I was suffering from some kind of reaction. My friends were all good to me and frequently included me in their family reunions and weekends. When the men I had known in France happened to be in England they introduced me to their wives and families. The hospitality extended to me was overwhelming. I went to every cinema and show in town. I had heard all about *Gone with the Wind* and as I had caught a glimpse of Vivien Leigh in Gibraltar, looking beautiful, that was the first film I saw. Nevertheless the days seemed to drag by. Everyone I knew was doing something except me.

I was still hoping Henri would join me, so I began looking for a small flat in London. There were plenty of vacancies in central London and I had the choice of three in the Piccadilly and St James Street area, all at the same rental. The two I did not choose were bombed to the ground. Mine escaped any war damage. Once more I had been lucky. The little flat was dirty and had to be painted throughout, and the parquet floor sanded and polished. When that was done I furnished it the best way I could. I bought pyjamas, slippers and a dressing-gown for Henri, guessing he would arrive without any personal belongings. I remember going to Soho and buying a bottle of French champagne and a French liqueur brandy to celebrate his arrival. When I opened them after the war the champagne bottle was filled with wine and the brandy bottle contained lolly water. I was not surprised to find the wine merchant had disappeared without leaving an address.

In the middle of October I had a terrible nightmare and woke up convinced Henri was dead. Micheline and another friend were staying with me at the time. I woke them up and told them of my fears. They both pointed out that it was foolish to allow a nightmare to upset me in this manner but the doubt I had in my mind continued for days, until at last

I thought that I was being unrealistic.

I first met Richard Broad in Marseille, when as a lieutenant in the Seaforth Highlanders he had managed to escape from the Occupied Zone with his men. We met again in London and I happened to mention that I was becoming bored with so much spare time on my hands. The only thing I wanted to do was to return to France, as I felt sure Henri would not join me in London. I cannot say truthfully whether I believed him to be dead or alive. It is quite possible that I believed in my heart that he was dead, but as I hoped this was not correct I put all thought of the nightmare in the back of my mind. In any case, it had nothing to do with my desire to return to France as I knew I would have to wait until after the war before returning to Marseille.

The fact was that I had ceased to be amused by pub crawls, the endless rounds of clubs and the people I encountered in London. After all, being the capital of England it was where thousands of servicemen and women came on their leave passes, and it was natural they would want to enjoy themselves. I agreed with their aims, but in my case I was doing it every day.

Many of the Frenchmen I had met in Spain were in London and they were all joining the Free French Movement and going back to France for General de Gaulle's outfit. I did not want to return to France for the British so I requested an appointment with Colonel Passy at the Free French Headquarters. I was unaware of the intrigue going on at a high level between the British and the Free French. How could I know? I had been in the field where we helped each other. To my bitter disappointment Colonel Passy declined my services. It was a great blow, as the loyalty I felt for France was deep and sincere.

The next day I received a call from an official in the Intelligence Service (he was known to me) who asked me bluntly what I had been doing at General de Gaulle's headquarters. I denied the charge but when he described the clothes I had worn and other particulars of my appointment I agreed that he was correct. Everything fell into place. The British were spying on the French, who were probably taking me for a British stooge.

Nancy's Maquis identity card.

The Maquis (above) *embarking for battle and* (below) *preparing for a raid on Gestapo headquarters at Montluçon in June 1944. The raid was successful; the whole operation took 12 minutes.*

In the meantime Richard had suggested voluntary work in the canteen of the Combined Operations Headquarters in Whitehall. They were short of staff so I agreed to give them four hours a day. It was a mistake. I think I was the only commoner in my section. It was definitely not the place for someone with my background, my down-to-earth views and forthright manner. All the titled ladies would come in and have long chats about their mutual friends before doing one scrap of work. I kept my temper, and my place, because I liked Richard and did not wish to embarrass him as he had recommended me. I heard 'darling Dickie' (Mountbatten) had left Europe and 'darling Bob' (Laycock) had taken over. The way these women gushed made me positively ill. I was relieved when I had a good reason to leave.

It was either Richard Broad or Ian Garrow who put me in touch with Special Operations Executive. SOE was secretly formed in 1940 especially to work with the Resistance forces in German-occupied Europe. I went for an interview and in due course I was accepted and started my training. At last I was on the way back to France. First of all we were sent to a school outside London for three days. I was not surprised it was called 'The Mad House' by all the students. I suppose there was a good reason for doing some of the exercises they invented. The obstacle course was confusing, as each student, unknown to the others, had different instructions. It was no good to try and cheat by following the leader.

Searching an imaginary room for hidden imaginary papers has never been my forte, so I probably failed that test. But it was the psychiatrist who really got on my nerves. After all, the profession was not as popular in 1943 as it is today. He showed me a piece of paper with a big blot of ink on it and asked me what I could see. When I said I saw a blot of ink he got quite agitated and tried to put words in my mouth. He was a New Zealander. I told him he should be doing something constructive instead of wasting his time and mine. A fellow student told me afterwards that she had told him she had seen dragons instead of ink blots. She had got this piece of advice from a previous student. I suppose I failed that test too.

We were to leave for a course of six weeks in Scotland. Richard took me to lunch at Monseignor's after which I reported back to Welbeck House, ready to leave that evening. A Frenchwoman going on the same course was having a row with one of the instructors, Denis Rake, and tried to enlist my support. Denis had worked in the field in France, so naturally I took his side. I liked Denis but could not be bothered with petty squabbles, so I refused to be involved. One thing led to another, most of the problems being caused by the French-woman, and before long I was in trouble with one of the staff. Unfortunately his approach was all wrong. He was not a good judge of character, otherwise he would not have spoken to me the way he did. I told him what he could do and where he could put it, and he fired me on the spot. His name was Selwyn Jepson. We did not like each other. He was so sarcastic I decided he either had an ulcer or was constipated.

I rang up Richard to tell him I had already been sacked. He remarked on the brevity of my employment but took me out to dinner to cheer me up. The next morning I resolved to find out some way of joining the Free French. I had two friends in London working on the General's staff. I confided in them and we put our heads together and planned our course of action. Unfortunately, or fortunately, before they had time to get any results, I was re-employed by SOE. I never knew what went on behind the scenes.

I was sent on the next course to Scotland. No other females, just men. Weeks later, Colonel Buckmaster, the head of the French Section of SOE, told me I had been lucky to have been taken off the previous course as it had been subjected to one friction after another. I could well believe it. That particular French girl was a born mischief-maker.

As for me, I determined that from that moment on I would keep to myself as much as possible. I would remain aloof from my fellow students and the staff. It was a bit of a strain and only lasted a few days, because the men I was with were all so pleasant and friendly. Our group consisted mainly of French, with several French Canadians, two Poles and myself. Most of them were just as fun-loving as I was. The house we lived in was in a lovely part of Scotland, Inverie Bay. Although we had to work hard we always found time to relax. We were a good team.

We were instructed in the handling of explosives and

grenades, weapons and silent killing. I had never held a revolver in my hand, let alone a Bren gun or a grenade, so this expert training was essential for me. We had day and night manoeuvres; it rained most of the time and we came back soaking wet and covered in mud. There was always plenty of hot water, and dry clothes waiting for us. The instructors were patient and the staff pampered us.

We were taken over to 'Eilean n'a Breac' (The Island of the Sea Trout). An experienced deep-sea fisherman had been detailed to teach us how to retrieve parachutes and containers that had fallen in the water. This man was still alive several years ago when some close friends of mine were trout fishing in the area. He was reminiscing about his forty years at sea and said with good-humoured disgust that he'd never fallen in the sea until he met me!

I'd fallen overboard and when the chaps tried to pull me out of the water I laughed so much I eventually overturned the boat. It was a case of swim or drown for everyone, including the poor fisherman.

That's definitely one course I didn't pass.

I'd been thoroughly enjoying myself during those weeks in Scotland, except for the first days when because of that creep Selwyn Jepson I had been pretending to be prim and proper. Then we overheard that some big brass were coming up from London to see how we were getting on, and the school's CO was preparing our reports. Remembering all the mischief I'd been up to with some of the group, I was immediately filled with remorse and began to worry about my report card. I decided that by hook or by crook I had to see it before the big brass did.

My friend Raymond was all for my plan (which obviously had to be done by crook!) but he didn't relish the idea of being caught red-handed. As I was desperate, we decided that Raymond would be the lookout, I'd do the rest, and as a reward I'd also read his report card.

Soon afterwards I ambled into the office with a query, and when the clerk's back was turned I made an impression in plasticine of the key I hoped was the right one. Raymond and I made our duplicates. We'd been taught to do all these things at the school, so why not make the most of it?

105

That night, when everything was quiet, and with Raymond mounting guard, I found that the key fitted. I glanced at our reports. Raymond's was good, and there was nothing in mine which upset me; on the contrary—I read with surprise that I had been 'good for morale'.

From then on 'Miss Prim and Proper' vanished forever and 'Miss Exuberant' resumed her rightful place.

I have no idea what I would have said had I been caught, but when I was young I never believed in crossing bridges before it was time.

After six weeks we made our way to Ringway, near Manchester, to be instructed in the art of parachuting.

At the parachute school there were dozens of groups of students, of all nationalities, emanating from a variety of training courses and destined for service with different organisations. The groups were not encouraged to intermix socially for obvious security reasons. We always kept very much to ourselves.

I hated the pre-parachuting exercises. To my mind it was an excellent way of breaking some bones which would prevent the much more important parachuting jump into France. My fellow trainees kept me up to the mark. They had noticed a French girl in another group and they were determined I should outshine her at all costs. I certainly did not have the faith in myself that they did, but when they threatened me with a fate worse than death I did my best to justify their confidence.

All our meals were served in a huge dining-hall. The commanding officer and his staff sat at a long table running the full width of the room, with their backs to the wall and facing their students. The students were seated at both sides of several long tables running lengthwise, from the top table to the other end of the room. Thus the staff were in a position to observe everything that occurred in the dining-hall.

One morning at the breakfast table an American sergeant sitting opposite me passed me a small packet, saying that it was a present. Although Raymond Bachelor sitting on my right whispered in French not to accept it, I did so, thinking it was chewing gum or chocolate. I knew what a French letter meant in English, just as I knew the French name for it, but I

106

did not know what a condom was until I opened the packet and saw three of them lying there together with the instructions.

I don't know what reaction the American expected, especially at a breakfast table. There was silence all round me. Then I proceeded to read out the instructions, much to the amusement of everyone at our table except the American who, red in the face, left the table. I put them in the pocket of my battle dress and continued eating my breakfast. As we left the dining-hall the CO called me to one side, apologised for the behaviour of the American and offered to disembarrass me of the unmentionables. He was surprised when I declined his offer, adding that they might come in handy later on. We never saw the American again. He vanished. I feel sure he was reprimanded.

We did our parachute jumps and the first one was the worst. The others were exhilarating, but when the weather was too bad for the planes and we jumped from a static balloon, I swore I would never do it again. Unfortunately, the bad weather continued and we had one more night jump before the course finished. We were given the choice of waiting for the weather to clear or jumping from a balloon. I was all for waiting for fine weather but my group wanted to have a weekend in London. Threatening me was no good; this time they bribed me, each one promising me a double whisky in a club in London. Jumping from a balloon on a pitch-black night, when all is silent and the parachute takes longer to open than it does from a plane, will never be my favourite pastime. As I glided down I thought I should have stipulated trebles.

We enjoyed a week's well-earned leave in London. By now so deep was our friendship we spent nearly all our waking hours together. I introduced them to all the pubs and clubs where I was known and they were able to appreciate the hospitality of the genuine Londoner and the people who lived there normally, whose courage and humour never faltered during those perilous years and was to become a legend. Naturally there was a seamy side to the city, but we only patronised the establishments where everything was above-board where we could enjoy good clean fun.

Our next course was the security school. It was held at Beaulieu in the New Forest near Bournemouth. Here we were joined by other students although I was still the only female. We were there for three weeks. It was a worthwhile course and we learnt a great deal of valuable information. Unfortunately one instructor, who lectured on matters pertaining to the German forces, was hard to follow. He had a habit of saying 'N'est-ce pas' in every second sentence during his lecture of forty-five minutes. We found ourselves listening for the phrase instead of learning how to identify German tanks and military vehicles, the ranks of officers and the divisional flashes on their uniforms.

Eventually we ran a guessing competition. During his next lecture every student in the room looked at him attentively, at the same time noting surreptitiously the number of times he said 'N'est-ce pas'. After his lecture we added up our strokes. He had said it over 180 times and was known afterwards as 'Monsieur N'est-ce pas'.

Each instructor would hang his big blackboard on the wall facing the class. After his lecture he would leave and the following instructor would remove the board and replace it with a clean one. I had a brilliant idea which was endorsed by every student. I sacrificed one of my condoms and a Canadian blew it up and tied it with a piece of string. We installed it behind the blackboard minutes before 'Monsieur N'est-ce pas' arrived. He was not a cheerful character. As a matter of fact he always seemed to be on the surly side. He took down the blackboard and out bounced our work of art! He turned to the class and with a look of disgust advised the person responsible for such vulgar behaviour to remove the offending object. We all looked innocent. I was in the front row and it was especially hard for me to keep a straight face.

Halfway through his lecture the senior officer in charge of security came into the classroom, presumably to see how the lecture was progressing. As he opened the door the draught from the open window lifted up our balloon and it bounced all over the floor in front of him. The instructor carried on with his lecture, the colonel sat down as if nothing had happened, and we withheld our laughter until the lunch break. The fact that I possessed these articles would have been passed on by the parachute school, so they probably said to themselves, 'One gone, two to go.' I know they searched my room because I used to place little pieces of sewing cotton on my underclothes in the chest of drawers, and they were always being disturbed.

While we were at Beaulieu a delightful instructor, Captain Clarke, taught us how to poach game if we were short of food in France. He was the chief gamekeeper at Sandringham. Every now and again he would scratch his head and say he didn't know what on earth His Majesty would say when he found out about his lectures.

Another instructor whom we all liked very much taught us, amongst other things, codes and how to describe or identify a person by remembering any unusual features, noticeable mannerisms or a distinct way of standing or walking. We knew him as Captain Walker. He was always pleasant to us but in our company we felt there was a certain nervousness on his part. Perhaps he had good cause, as our group led the way when any mischief was brewing.

We were not allowed visitors under any circumstances but one of the new arrivals was a charming young officer, known to us as John, whom we guessed would have relations in England. Therefore we invited him to assist us in our next unofficial exercise. Captain Walker was to be the target. We were going to test his own powers of observation the very next afternoon. Raymond Bachelor dressed up in my clothes, with my high-heeled shoes, make-up and a silk scarf worn as a turban to hide his short hair. We were waiting in the garden for Captain Walker to give us a practical demonstration of a police line-up.

When he arrived he saw the 'girl' crossing the lawn to talk to John. Instantly one could feel the 'hackles rise on the bloodhound'! What was a strange woman doing on our lawn? I told him it was John's sister come to visit him, which made him more agitated. One could feel that John was up for a court martial. All this time Raymond had been talking and laughing with 'her brother', throwing his arms around and looking straight at Captain Walker, who crossed the lawn with me by his side. Then I piped up and said, 'Surely you recognise her, Captain Walker?' He did not. Only when he came face to face with Raymond did the penny drop. He was a good sport, he took it well and we all enjoyed a good laugh.

One night while an interrogation exercise was under way I noticed Captain Walker hang his forage cap in the hall, which was dark. I popped a condom in the back of it and he wore it for some time before it was brought to his attention. Not a word was spoken. However, my guess was they were now saying, 'Two gone, one to go.' But the third one I was keeping for something really outstanding. Besides, until the end of the course they would all be on tenterhooks.

This course was an intense one which entailed study and hard work, but our high spirits were never dampened. The harder we worked, the harder we played. Our particular group had grown slightly and we were about ten strong, including Hubert, a British Army officer, with whom I was to parachute into France.

After breakfast, and before activities commenced, we would stroll out into the garden and sit in the empty swimming pool, which was usually nice and sunny and sheltered from the wind. If our instructors thought we were studying our exercise books they were wrong. We were recording hundreds of risqué stories John used to narrate. He was a fantastic story-teller and had a fund of really juicy ones he never repeated except by request.

After dinner, unless a night exercise was arranged, we would gather in our lounge and drink pint after pint of draught bitter beer. We were not allowed spirits in this school and although the British enjoyed the bitter, the French boys and I did not. But we drank it just the same. When the batman in our lounge was about to go off duty he would ask for our last orders. Generally forty pints of bitter would be lined up along the shelf which ran the full length of one of the walls. Only when they were consumed would we bid each other goodnight. When we had our mess bills at the end of the course the CO of the school said that up until that time we held the record for the consumption of bitter.

Our security training was coming to an end. We had one more exercise to perform. We were to dress in civilian clothes, proceed to Bournemouth and carry out the instructions we had been given. Several instructors, including Captain Walker, would be placed at strategic points as observers. On no account were we to approach them or to give any sign of recognition.

As I completed the first part of my assignment I noticed Captain Walker, wearing his greatcoat, standing in an arcade and looking anxious as if he were waiting for someone. The second time I approached the arcade I did not pass him. I went straight up to him and threw my arms around his neck, saying how happy I was to see him after all the years, and cunningly attached the last of my precious condoms to the back of his greatcoat. He stood there in full view of the passers-by until the exercise was over. At long last SOE could rest in peace!

The main training courses were over but there were still a couple of three-day ones to come. The first one taught us how to make home-made explosives with ingredients readily available in France, either at a chemist's or a hardware store. It was at this school that I met Violette Szabo, whose story was later told in both the book and the film *Carve Her Name with Pride*. Not only was she very beautiful, but she was great fun. We never lost an opportunity to get up to some mischief at that school. Our greatest achievement by far was to de-bag an instructor and hoist his pants on a flagpole. Violette and I became very friendly and saw a lot of each other in London. A couple of the boys in my group fell madly in love with her and the four of us would enjoy the night life in London whenever we were free. Violette was later ambushed in France and executed at Ravensbruck. I was very sad when I was told this after the war—but by then I had lost so many friends.

The last exercise was probably planned to give us the confidence to travel with false identity cards. We were given a false British identity card which our headquarters assured us would be accepted by any routine police inspection, together with a return railway warrant from London to whatever city we were assigned, plus £10. We were to imagine that England was occupied by an enemy and we were organising resistance in that particular city. There were a few stipulations. As soon as we had chosen our accommodation we had to telephone a certain number and say, 'I'm so and so and I'm at . . . .' At a given time we were to keep an appointment, holding in our hand a Penguin book. We were required to find out what a certain factory was manufacturing. We had to visit a man discreetly, the name and address of whom we had been given, with a view to enlisting him in the Resistance.

I prepared myself a good, simple cover story. I was supposed to be married to a British Army officer but since the fall of Singapore I did not know his whereabouts or whether he was dead or alive. I had one small boy, whose photograph I always kept on the dressing-table. We lived in London but he was afraid of the air raids and I was going to buy a small house in a quieter part of the country.

I went to Chester. It did not take me long to realise the local police were watching me. The telephone call had given them a head start. The appointment, which was in a pub, did not materialise so I left after ten minutes, guessing that someone was watching for any sign of nervousness on my part. Outside the factory that had been assigned to me was a notice 'Women Wanted'. I obtained a job immediately but left at lunch time without claiming pay. It was only making nails.

The man I had to interview was an important business executive. I had a valid reason for phoning him in his office. That was the only contact I made as I had to be careful not to compromise him. Remembering Henri and the way he found it impossible to look after his particular line of business and accept any regular or continuous resistance work, I resolved to be prudent in the way I used this man. He would be a tremendous asset to my organisation as long as I took every possible precaution not to compromise him, as he was well-known in Chester with excellent contacts and a good social standing. I discussed the matter with him and he said he would be delighted to fall in with my plans, and looked forward to being informed of the details at a later date.

I paid three guineas to an estate agent and became a registered would-be house buyer, stating I would be willing to pay up to £2,000 for a small house somewhere on the outskirts of Chester. I feel guilty every time I think of that poor man chasing all over the countryside trying to make a sale.

The local police were hot on my tail but I managed to keep one step ahead. I knew someone was searching my room as all the little traps I placed in various spots were disturbed. The night before I was due to return to London a policeman called

112

at the hotel, asking that I meet him downstairs in the lobby. I refused point blank and informed the messenger that if he wanted to see me he would have to come to my room. I was questioned at great length and he appeared to be satisfied with my cover story. As he left he said he hoped that I would find a suitable house. I never knew whether or not this particular policeman was in on the secret, although the Chief of Police obviously was.

Back in London I was delighted to find that the rest of my group had not been so fortunate. They had all been whisked off to the police station, where after a short interrogation they had been released once they had given the police a certain telephone number to ring.

Our training was over, and Hubert and I were busy preparing for our mission to France. Personal codes (mine was an unsavoury limerick) to be registered, safe houses, contacts and cover stories all had to be memorised. This was no easy matter. I was to be Hélène to London, Andrée to the French, and had at least three other names for emergencies. At long last the day of our departure was confirmed and from then on it was one party after another with our little group.

We spent our last night at the Astor night-club in Park Lane. At four o'clock in the morning we did parachute rolls along Piccadilly to my flat, singing at the top of our voices 'Gory, gory, what a hell of a way to die'.

It was sad to leave our friends, especially for me because I had been with them for so long and we had become so close. There had never been one moment of dissension in all that time, just deep, sincere friendship, with each one helping the other. As I said goodbye, I realised how fortunate I had been.

CHAPTER NINE

Hubert and I were parachuted into France near Montluçon, and were taken to the nearby village of Cosne-d'Allier, where I did my meet-the-people in the village square.

I did not meet the farmer on whose property we had landed. Had the Germans made any enquiries regarding the activity so close to his farmhouse on the night in question, he wanted to be able to say he had gone to bed early and had not heard any strange noises.

Although we would have been happier and felt safer away from Cosne-d'Allier, we were waiting for someone called Hector to contact us, as he was our only link to Gaspard, the leader of the Maquis d'Auvergne. This was the group we were to work with, but we had to be taken to them by an inter-mediary.

By now I had given Hubert a watered-down version of my social début in the village and he was even more anxious to find another place to live. We discussed the pros and cons fully and agreed we would wait another day, but miraculously Hector arrived the next morning. Trouble in his own area had been the cause of his delay.

There was no bathroom in this old house and I had been washing myself from neck to knee in a tiny *cabinet de toilette*. I was tired of standing up in the cramped roomette, so I got a big basin, filled it with water, took it back to the bedroom, sat down and started to wash my feet, at the same time discussing our immediate plans with Hubert. My revolver was by my side.

In walked Hector, who took one look at me, my feet and my revolver and laughed for at least two minutes. Actually neither of us thought it was very amusing but perhaps the long delay we had experienced had made us lose our sense of humour. Every time he recounts this tale my feet get bigger and the basin gets smaller, and the last time I heard the story I had a Bren gun by my side!

114

We were greatly relieved to see him in spite of the fact that he did not have the information or addresses we required, but as he promised to send them with his courier in two days' time we were both happy to think our troubles were over.

Our happiness was short-lived as the courier did not arrive. And we did not see Hector again until after the war. He was arrested, survived Buchenwald and now lives on the outskirts of Paris. Sadly we had to face the cold truth. For the time being we were up the proverbial creek without a paddle. Hubert and I both decided we would have to forget all about security and confide to a certain extent in our host Jean and his wife. This done, he thought he might be able to find Laurent's hideout. Laurent was one of the leaders of a local Maquis group, and he would be able to take us to Gaspard, who was in charge of all the separate groups of the Maquis in the area.

We started out early in the morning in Jean's *gazogène* (a charcoal-fuelled car). He seemed to know all the secondary roads extremely well and assured us there was not much danger of running into the Germans. We looked at each other in silence as we had been briefed in London only to travel by bicycle or train, or better still on foot. Hubert was white in the face; as for me, once again I decided I was going to play it by ear.

Jean drove from one contact to another until, when it was late evening, we found Laurent. I was always grateful to Jean and his wife for delivering us into the safe hands of Laurent, who was a tall, handsome man. When I knew him better we became great friends. I respected him, too, because he was a man who knew no fear. He conducted us to an old château near Saint-Flour in the Cantal and went to inform Gaspard of our arrival.

The purpose of our mission was to meet Gaspard, who was believed to have three to four thousand men hiding in the departments of the Allier, Puy-de-Dôme, Haute Loire and Cantal. We were to make our own assessment not only of the leader Gaspard, but also of the manner in which his con-siderable army had been formed and was now being operated and controlled. If we felt reasonably sure that he and his Maquis would be an asset to the Allies when and after they landed on D-day, then the French Section of SOE, commanded by Colonel Buckmaster in England would assist them with finance and arms.

Laurent had been gone for days before Gaspard arrived at the château and our meeting was not a happy one. He maintained he had no knowledge of Hector and had therefore not been expecting any assistance from SOE. He did not inform us that he was hoping for the support of an Inter-Allied team, a fact that London, for reasons of their own, had failed to mention in our briefings.

If Hubert and I had possessed all the cards in the pack we would not have wasted the time we did when we first landed. It was also unfortunate that, owing to the arrest of Hector, we had not received the detailed local information promised to us in London. The fact that our wireless operator chose to spend some time with a friend before joining us did not diminish our problems.

Hubert and I had the good fortune to overhear the group discussing us while they were sitting in the big kitchen where they congregated all the time. They seemed sure we had some money and they were plotting to relieve me of it and get rid of me at the same time. At a later period when Gaspard and I had more respect for each other he assured me the men had been joking. That could be true, but when I am stranded in an old, empty château, many kilometres from civilisation, surrounded by a gang of unshaven, disreputable-looking men, I tend to be cautious and take things seriously.

Without any radio contact with London we were not in an enviable position, so when Gaspard suggested he would send us to Chaudes-Aigues in the Cantal, where a man called Henri Fournier was in charge of the local Maquis, we readily agreed.

In retrospect I can guess why Gaspard adopted the attitude he did. He was banking on the support of the Inter-Allied group but in the event it did not materialise he did not want to antagonise us irreparably. We were of no use to him without a radio and the money, which we said (quite untruthfully) we did not possess. He would kill two birds with one stone. He would dispatch us to a man he disliked who would have us on his hands if we failed to become functional. When many years had passed, after reading information that was gradually coming to light, I concluded that Gaspard had been under the misapprehension that an elaborate military scheme involving a French airborne force being dropped in the Massif Central area but D-day would become operational. It did not materialise, probably another case of the left hand not letting the right hand know what it was doing.

In normal times Henri Fournier was an executive in hotel management. He detested the Germans and he and his wife had come to live in Chaudes-Aigues for the duration of the Occupation. He was puzzled by our arrival but when we explained the situation I think the mystery was clarified because, when we became friends, he admitted to me in confidence that he heartily disliked Gaspard.

Fournier arranged accommodation for us in a funny little hotel high up in the hills, in a village called Lieutades. It was freezing cold, both inside the hotel and outside, and there was little to eat. We had absolutely nothing to do and we were both beginning to worry as our radio operator, Denis Rake, was long overdue.

Denis (or Denden, as he was called) had been one of our instructors at SOE school, the one arguing with the French-woman. Even in those days when homosexuality was illegal he had never concealed the fact that he was queer. Indeed it was always the first thing he mentioned, especially to women, who often found him too attractive for his liking. We were both fond of him but knew he could be completely unreliable.

Denden arrived by car just as we were beginning to give up hope. He found me sitting on the wall of the local cemetery and wanted to know if I was picking a suitable grave! He realised that his late arrival had caused us needless anxiety and in true Denden fashion he told us a cock-and-bull story which neither of us believed. However, a radio operator is an important person in the field, and we were not going to give him a reason to leave us and go straight back to his lover, which was exactly where he had been. On landing in France by Lysander he had met the man he had been having an affair with several weeks before in London, and they had decided to have a last fling.

Nevertheless, we were absolutely delighted to see him for

now we could put our plans into action. While waiting for Denden we had decided that if he did arrive we would help Fournier first of all. We had been impressed by what we had seen of his group. We respected him and knew that he had spent a lot of his savings on the Resistance. We packed our bags and left for Chaudes-Aigues.

Fournier was overwhelmed with joy when told that we would shortly be in radio contact with London and that his group would be the first to receive our report. He and Hubert were busy making out the lists of weapons and explosives they hoped would be sent from England, and Denden and I were busy coding the messages to be transmitted.

When the day and hour of the transmission arrived the room was full of Maquisards anxious to witness this exciting event. They appeared to be making Denden nervous so I asked them to leave the room. Reluctantly they filed out, all except Fournier, who refused to budge. Denden looked more nervous than before. He told me why. He was transmitting on the wrong schedule. He was twenty-four hours too soon. The three of us managed to restrain our laughter and started the proceedings all over again the following day. There were no more hitches and soon we were preparing for our first operation.

The plateaux on top of the mountains which surround Chaudes-Aigues were ideal for air-drops. Fournier and his group had surveyed the whole area and were of the opinion that we could receive, unpack and distribute the contents of the containers on the field and return to our homes without any interference. As soon as London had received our messages and we were all organised we received air-drops on six consecutive nights. It continued to be a roaring success until later on when Gaspard arrived with his men and was followed almost immediately by the Germans.

We manned the fields from ten at night until four in the morning, unless the planes arrived beforehand. We would unpack the containers immediately. The weapons had to be cleaned and all the protective grease removed before we handed them over to the leaders of the individual groups. Every available man assisted. Nevertheless, sometimes it would be noon before we finished and after lunch before we could

118

Maquisards receiving weapons training.

A group of happy Maquisards who have just chased the Germans out of a town in August 1944. Nancy is third from the left, holding a poodle.

The Château de Fragnes, home of Nancy's Maquis group.

Nancy, Denden (centre) *and John Alsop* (rear) *discover the château's wine cellar.*

snatch a few hours' sleep. It was a strenuous time for everyone; we were kept on the go continuously, but it was also rewarding to witness the enthusiasm of Fournier and his Maquis.

Every now and then Hubert, Denis and I would receive parcels from London which would arrive in a special container. Words cannot describe the thrill it gave me to open mine, stamped all over with 'Personal for Hélène'. Here we were, in the middle of a war, high up in the mountains of Central France, yet because of the thoughtfulness of SOE Headquarters we felt close to London.

My parcel always contained personal items unobtainable in France during the Occupation, plus supplies of Lizzie Arden's products, Brooke Bond tea, chocolates or confectionery. Without fail there'd be a note and a small gift from Claire Wolfe, the only girl I'd been friendly with at headquarters. We remained staunch friends, and when she died at her home on the Isle of Man in 1984 I was grief-stricken.

Once, to my delight, I received a letter from my old pal, Richard Broad. I remember jumping up and down shouting, 'I've got a letter from R.B.!' Hubert and Denis weren't a bit interested—they'd never heard of him! But I kissed every page as I read the letter. I still have it—and it's still covered in lipstick.

I was thankful that Hubert and I had arranged the tasks we would perform to our mutual satisfaction. He would deal with all matters of a military nature and meet Gaspard whenever necessary and possible. I would be in charge of finance and its distribution to the group leaders. I would visit the groups, assess the merit of their demands and arrange for their airdrops, which we would both attend if possible. The tables had turned. After being regarded as a bloody nuisance by Gaspard when I first arrived, I now carried a lot of weight. *I* was the one who decided which groups were to get arms and money. Denden was in charge of coding and decoding the messages he transmitted and received. German detectors looking for illegal transmitters had to be evaded, and when we were expecting a message from London about a drop of arms, we listened to the five BBC news broadcasts a day. It was time-consuming, exacting work.

For my part, I had found a different attitude in France when

I returned and joined the Maquis. By the spring of 1944 anyone with a brain could see that the Allies would beat the Germans and consequently some French people were already preparing to play politics. This exasperated me as the memory of the colossal harm caused by politics in the thirties still rankled. The majority of the men wanted to kick the Germans out of their country, return to their homes and pick up the threads of their lives. Liberation was on the horizon; now it was no longer a battle between 'cops and robbers', it was becoming a battle of wits.

When Fournier told me Colonel Gaspard was promoted to general. I snorted and Fournier laughed. Hubert was inclined to be impressed and a little in awe of rank. I was not. Not that I did not respect genuine rank, but in the Resistance, especially in the Maquis, some of them upgraded themselves in such a fashion that the chap you met one week as a soldier or civilian suddenly appeared as a colonel a few days later. If you enquired about such a rapid promotion you would be given the name of someone you had never heard of, or the initials of some secret organisation equally unknown to you. Furthermore, the alleged promotion would be promulgated after the Liberation. Some of the newly promoted officers tried to pull rank on me.

Fournier laughed when I told him what I wanted to do. In view of the importance of my department—finance and air-drops—I promoted myself to the rank of field marshal, to be promulgated after the war! No one would pull rank on me and get away with it. I continued to arm and assist, to the best of my ability, the worthwhile and dedicated groups in the Maquis, irrespective of the rank of their leaders.

During May, as a direct outcome of the large concentration of men in the mountains, a continuity of pitched battles were being fought between the Germans and our Maquis d'Auvergne. The Maquisards defended themselves brilliantly. Although they were always outnumbered by the enemy, sometimes comprising crack SS troops, the losses inflicted on the Germans were staggering. A few days before the Allies landed in Normandy the Germans attacked Gaspard's group in Mont Mouchet. They were stopped by the Maquis and driven back in defeat.

It was soon clear that the Germans were becoming concerned about the steadily increasing strength and actions of the Maquis. It was either just before or after this battle that the traitor Roger the Légionnaire was in our region. He and another German agent had managed to infiltrate Gaspard's Maquis, stating they wished to join his group. Their story and their odd behaviour aroused suspicions almost immediately, and in the cross-firing which subsequently took place, one Maquisard was killed and both German agents were seriously wounded. Roger received three bullets in the chest from a Colt .45 but as he was wearing a bullet-proof vest he did not die immediately. Interrogated under extreme pressure, he confessed to having been responsible for initiating a series of unbelievably inhuman punishments inflicted on captured members of the Resistance. He also stated that he had been directly responsible for the arrest of O'Leary at Toulouse on 2 March 1943. His confessions were taken down and I was given a copy to forward to London. Shortly afterwards Roger and the other German agent were shot and buried on Mont Mouchet.

I shivered when I read the report. One of the Resistance members Roger was seeking was the person who obtained the arms from England. Little did he know that he had passed me as he drove along the narrow mountain track. It was unbelievable that I had missed him in Toulouse and been so close to him on this mountain.

I left the area as soon as possible. I could understand the hatred the Maquisards had for the Germans who behaved like crazed wild animals in their dealings with the Resistance. I hated and loathed them too but personally I favoured an accurate bullet and a quick death. Nevertheless there is a lot to be said for the proverb 'an eye for an eye', and when all is said and done Roger was only paying for some of the abominable treatment meted out to his victims. Torture is horrible. But before any outsiders form an opinion they should study both sides of the story closely.

On 4 June 1944 I received a special message from London stating that 'Anselm' was being dropped that night in the Montluçon area, in the *département* of the Allier, and I was ordered to collect him. That was easier said than done. Hector had been arrested before he had time to give us details of safe houses, contacts and passwords. I knew that a Madame Renard was one of the contacts and I thought I had heard that she had been the housekeeper of an ambassador in Paris and also that she made good cakes.

Fournier gave me his best car and driver plus a bicycle which we put on the roof. The area between Chaudes-Aigues and Montluçon was swarming with Germans and Maquis each thirsting for revenge. In those days the only petrol-driven cars belonged to either the Germans or the Resistance. We were inclined to be more afraid of the Maquis than we were of the Germans because some Maquisards had been known to shoot first and ask questions afterwards. We didn't want them to mistake us for the enemy.

However, all went well. We enquired at each village along our route as to the whereabouts of Germans and Maquisards and, thanks to the help and information given us, we reached Montluçon safely. We hid the car in some bushes and my driver concealed himself a little distance away so he could observe anyone who discovered our vehicle.

I had promised one of the men in my group that I would call on his wife who was pregnant. She was happy to have news of her husband but had never heard of a Madame Renard. She did give me the name and address of a friend who, she said, might be able to help. I cycled to her home. Although the name Renard did not ring a bell, when I mentioned the fact that she had been in the employ of an ambassador she was able to help me trace her. The town was full of Germans and there were patrols and road-blocks everywhere.

Madame Renard opened the door when I rang. I tried to explain as best I could the predicament I was in and how I had found her. She just stood there staring at me intently. Suddenly I could smell rum baba and I told her I knew all about her cakes. She laughed and led me into the kitchen. She called to 'Anselm', who came out of a cupboard pointing a Colt .45 clutched in his hand. We looked at each other in astonishment. It was René Dusacq, whom I had met during my training in England. He was also one of the men who had kissed me goodbye when I left on my mission. He was to become known as Bazooka.

Dusacq nearly passed out when I said we would be going by car to Chaudes-Aigues. He sat in the back with his Colt at the ready, while I was in the front with the driver, a couple of Sten guns and half a dozen grenades. It was a smooth trip back to our headquarters where, to my bitter disappointment, I learnt that during my absence the Allies had landed and I had missed all the fun of blowing up our targets.

On 10 June the Germans attacked Mont Mouchet, this time supported by over 11,000 troops, with artillery, tanks and armoured cars, as against Gaspard's 3,000 Maquisards with light arms. Incredibly, they captured an armoured car and two cannons. During the night the Germans withdrew which gave the Maquis the opportunity to remove some of their vehicles, food and clothing over to our region. The attack recommenced at dawn. The Maquis were ordered to pull out at nightfall but in the meantime they fought like tigers. They were magnificent. The German losses were always anything from 4 to 10 per cent more than the casualties of the Maquis. Is it any wonder that the next time they attacked the Maquis d'Auvergne, they doubled their strength? I was destined to find myself in the centre of their mighty battle array. The wonder is that I was not captured or killed.

From our headquarters we could hear the sound of the battle raging. Alas, we could offer no assistance to our colleagues in arms. The nature of the terrain between our position and the Maquis under attack made it impossible. All through the day our scouts kept us informed of the fighting going on. All we could do was get on with our work.

It was unfortunate that hundreds of new recruits were streaming into our area, ready to be armed. Hubert and Fournier and his lieutenants had no time to worry about the conflict going on over the mountain. They were trying desperately to interview, however briefly, and arm the new recruits. It was a fantastic sight. The men were coming into Chaudes-Aigues from all directions. Not even the sound of the fighting nearby dampened their enthusiasm.

Denden was forever coding and decoding; not only for the night operation but for the daylight parachutage from 150 planes we had been promised. I had been designated to the footwear department! Every man had to be fitted with one pair of British army boots and two pairs of socks. When the supplies in the village ran out I went up to the plateau and opened more containers. As soon as they had been fitted with boots they were passed on to Bazooka, who all day long and far into the night would be instructing them on how to use our weapons.

Gaspard and his men arrived soon after their battle with the Germans and installed themselves on top of one of the plateaux surrounding Chaudes-Aigues. Hubert tried diplomatically to get him to form his men into smaller groups but Gaspard waved aside the suggestion. He was rightly proud of the way he and his men had faced up to the German attack but he was a stubborn man and very self opinionated.

We were receiving more and more air-drops. Night after night the planes would fly over our plateau and drop our precious containers. We were so occupied unpacking them, degreasing and assembling the weapons before distributing them we had little time for sleep, but the atmosphere of the Maquisards with whom we were in daily contact was so exhilarating and gratifying that we never worried. I don't think any of the reception committees ever got over the thrill of seeing the parachutes drop from the planes. Least of all Fournier, who never missed a drop and who made sure that his men were in position at the correct time. It was bitterly cold on the plateau and from ten at night the ground would be soaking wet with the heavy dew. We used to soak loaf sugar in *eau de vie* (plum brandy) and suck them to try to keep warm.

Now that Gaspard was a 'General' he proceeded to turn the little village of Saint-Martial (I seem to remember it had been deserted by its inhabitants) into a pukka headquarters. He had a colonel from the regular Army with him on his staff, who had brought his wife with him. The colonel obviously had not forgotten the regular eating hours in the officers' mess and he introduced the same system in their headquarters. We had been used to eating when it was convenient and thought this was a bit of a joke. I kept out of the way and continued to eat in Chaudes-Aigues if possible.

Hubert attended the 'mess meals' on several days and begged me to at least put in an appearance. For the sake of peace I agreed to accompany him the next day. The 'general' sat at one end of the table, the colonel at the other end next to his wife, and the British and American members with the other French leaders were seated in between. I thought I heard someone address the colonel's wife as 'Madame la Colonel' and decided I must be mistaken, but after a while I realised they really were addressing her in this manner. That was enough for me. The Maquis and the way we were forced to live did not merit such French Army formality. Denden, Bazooka and I always found excuses to be too occupied at noon to join the 'High Command', as we called them, and soon Hubert followed suit whenever he could. He knew that with us at least he would have a laugh.

In spite of the danger and hard work we were enjoying working together with Fournier and his men. We all pulled together and there was never any friction between us. We could not say the same about Gaspard. We agreed unanimously that he was an extremely difficult man to get along with. I must admit that I personally never had any trouble with him after the first meeting. He may not have liked to admit it but he had met his match with me. And I intended to keep it that way.

I was glad to have René Dusacq with us. Although we had not yet received any bazookas, they were his favourite weapon after his Colt .45, which never left his side; hence his nickname. Also he helped me keep Denden under control. When I returned from visiting other groups an irate farmer came to see me, stating that his son had complained about an alleged advance from Denden. I managed to calm him down but it was embarrassing for our team. We had to be so careful the way we handled Denden because we knew he was just itching for an excuse to go and join his current lover further north. Bazooka, like us, was fond of him, but we could not close our eyes to the problems which would arise if we let him run wild amongst the good-looking young men in the Maquis. The trouble with Denden was that he actually believed most men were homosexual and if they were not, then they should be!

It always amuses me when I look back on those days with Denden. I often wonder why London decided to send him with us. Did they think our mission so hopeless it did not matter whom they sent? Did they think I was some kind of 'Den Mother'? This much I do know. Not many heterosexual men from SOE headquarters would have cared to go into the midst

125

of 7,000 full-blooded Maquisards with a self-proclaimed homosexual. They owe us a special debt of gratitude that, because of our understanding and handling of the affair, there were no court cases after the war, and that Denden was not torn to pieces or, alternatively, shot to death by an irate father.

Apart from that particular problem we were a happy team with Fournier, when he could get away from his nagging wife. We would laugh about the antics of the would-be politicians and others seeking power after the Liberation. For my part I always admired the men, so many of whom had been forced to leave their families unprovided for, either to escape the *relève* or the Germans. To me they will always represent the true spirit of the Resistance.

More and more recruits were joining Gaspard on the plateaux. The numbers of men assembling within the one area was getting completely out of control and our team felt it was courting trouble. Readily we agreed with Hubert's suggestion that we move further north. Unfortunately we had an air-drop that night and the next, plus our first daylight parachutage, in which we had been promised 150 planes. It had been so hard to organise and the arms would mean such a lot to the Maquis that we decided to postpone our departure for a few more days.

We came down from the plateau just before dawn, we were all exhausted and suffering from lack of sleep. Chaudes-Aigues has natural hot water springs so I went over to the public baths and soaked myself before popping into bed to snatch a few hours' sleep. It was not to be. The sound of gunfire made me leap out of bed. Hurriedly I dressed myself and raced down to the hall of the hotel where we lived.

The Germans were attacking us. Our look-outs came into the village to report. The whole area surrounding the mountains was literally swarming with Germans. When it was all over we learnt that they had been 22,000 strong, supported by over 1,000 vehicles, including tanks and armoured cars, trench mortars, artillery to back up the infantry, plus ten planes.

Several weeks previously I'd met Graham Buchanan, an Australian who'd been shot down near Nevers and rescued by a Maquis group. He was just as surprised as I was to meet another Australian in the French mountains.

From Nevers he and several other Allied airmen had been sent to Chaudes-Aigues where they were billetted in our hotel. I assured them there was nothing to worry about as I wished them goodnight. But a few hours later I had to tell them there was lots to worry about, that we were being attacked and would have to withdraw. Despite the panic and confusion which followed, all of this group eventually got back to England safely. (Graham Buchanan now lives near Murwillumbah in New South Wales, where he's a farmer.)

We packed as much as we could in our cars and raced up to Fridfont on the plateau to join the Maquis, which was 7,000 strong by now. Hubert left to confer with Gaspard who was on the other end of the plateau. He refused to consider withdrawal and stated he would fight to the death with his own group. I coded the message while Denden tried to contact London, not an easy thing to do when an operator's call is not expected. He persevered for hours and eventually received an instruction to transmit in one hour's time. Our message cancelled all our drops and requested Gaspard be ordered to withdraw.

Many of the containers had not been opened the night before as the planes had arrived late. I went along to the dropping zone and finished unpacking and putting the weapons in working order. Then I drove to all the positions where I could see our men, and once the arms and ammunition had been distributed I went back to Denden. We were the only two people not fighting. The men were holding back the onslaught and displaying outstanding bravery and enthusiasm as they defended the plateaux.

By now I was so exhausted I could hardly move. I was thirsty, hungry, sleepy and every bone in my body ached. As I could not help Denden until he received the final message from London I told him I was going to have a little kip and to wake me when I was needed.

I went to bed in a farmhouse where we had been authorised to take refuge. Just as I was dropping off to sleep Fournier came in and made me get up as he said it was too dangerous to stay inside. I was so sleepy I didn't care what happened. The only thing that would have wakened me completely was if I

127

had come face to face with a German. I slept for a couple of hours under a tree which I thought was just as dangerous and less comfortable than in the bed.

Finally, the message came through. We were all ordered to withdraw and a personal message for Gaspard ordered him to follow suit. Knowing how stubborn he could be, I asked Denden to sign the message as if coming from Konig, de Gaulle's General who led the Free French Forces of the Interior. I think the signature of a genuine General did the trick as Gaspard was as meek as a lamb when he took delivery of the signal.

Several planes bombed Saint-Martial as I left the village, and as my car became visible on the road to Fridfont one pilot of a Henschel left his group and started to chase my car. I could see his helmet and goggles as he banked to continue the pursuit, and I could hear the bullets whizzing as his aim got closer and closer. Suddenly a young Maquisard who was hiding in some bushes signalled me, shouting at the same time to jump. We flung ourselves into a culvert by the roadside as the plane flew overhead. The young man explained that Fridfont was being evacuated and that Bazooka was waiting for me further down the mountain. We dashed from cover to cover as the German pilot kept up the chase.

By the time I regained Fridfont everyone had been evacuated. Denden had already left with a group, Hubert with another. A young man who had waited for me conducted me to where my group was hiding and where I was delighted to find Bazooka. He always looked after me when he was around.

The withdrawal from the plateaux was a credit to the leaders of the Maquis. When the Germans arrived there was not a soul left. They must have felt very frustrated when, after the fierce fighting and their huge losses of life, they reached the top of the mountain only to find the entire Maquis had evaporated.

We had been formed into groups of fifty to 100, each one being led by one or two men familiar with the terrain we would be covering. Our leader had been a non-commissioned officer in the French Army. He originated from Alsace but although he was not a local man he was an experienced tracker so we had no qualms about getting lost in the tough mountains we would have to cross.

The Germans were patrolling all the bridges over the river Truyére which was deep, rapid and dangerous in most parts. They were also guarding closely any part of the river they thought we might attempt to cross. Thanks to Fournier and his men, we were able to cross the river in all the most dangerous places.

When Hubert and I first went to Chaudes-Aigues we were a little dubious about Fournier's suggestion that we use the plateaux as dropping zones, mainly because we were afraid we could get trapped by the Germans, without an escape route. It was then he showed us the ingenious scheme they had devised for crossing the river well away from bridges and secluded by heavy foliage.

They had installed layer after layer of heavy slabs of local stone on the river-bed and covered them by secured dead tree-trunks. They were not visible from above as they were at least 45 cm below the level of the water. All we had to do was remove our footwear, release the logs, balance ourselves with a walking stick or the branch of a tree, and cross in absolute safety. It worked perfectly.

Our destination was Saint-Santin, north-west of our present position. We headed south, crossed more mountains and gradually proceeded north in a round-about fashion. All the groups were taking different routes and we aimed to keep well away from each other whenever possible.

It took us about four days to reach Saint-Santin. It was tough going all the way. We were miles from the German infantry but their planes circled the entire region for days. They criss-crossed the area where we had been, dropping bombs, then systematically bombed all the surrounding mountains and forests hoping, presumably, to flush out the Maquisards, who luckily were not there.

After two days we were all thirsty and starving. We were out of immediate danger so we approached a prosperous-looking farm asking for water and a little food. They offered milk and food to 'L'anglaise', which I did not accept as they treated the bedraggled-looking men as if they were lepers. The poorer farmers and their wives gave as much food as they could spare and let us sleep in their barns overnight. I could not help thinking of the old saying, 'The rich get richer and the poor get poorer'.

At last we reached our destination. We ran into Gaspard and his group. I will always remember this meeting with him. He looked at me and said, 'Alors, Andrée', took my arm and walked the rest of the way with me and Bazooka. I do not know what he was thinking at that moment but for my part it was something special, as if from then on we would understand each other. He was a man of few words, and I knew from those two that he respected me as a comrade-in-arms.

From the information London had been able to give us at our briefings we got the impression that the German garrisons in the Auvergne were manned by elderly men and puny boys. I don't know what happened to them, perhaps they were too tired or too weak to take part in the conflict. We only saw crack German troops plus some mighty tough Mongol warriors who cared for little else but slaughter and plundering. Some of them were found lying on the battlefields with their pockets full of watches and human fingers with gold wedding-rings still on them. Nevertheless, hundreds and hundreds of the enemy lay wounded and over 1,400 were dead. The Maquis lost over a hundred and about the same number were wounded. What a glorious victory for Gaspard and his Maquis d'Auvergne, but from then on the Germans would be all out for revenge.

About thirty of us installed ourselves in an unfinished house on the outskirts of Saint-Santin. It belonged to the parents of a good-looking young man in our group on whom Denden had designs. Therefore, Bazooka, who was never without his Colt .45, was detailed to watch over this young man's honour.

For several days groups of men kept arriving with exciting tales of their long cross-country hike. Denden turned up, footsore and weary, without his transmitter, which he had buried, or his codes, which he had destroyed. We were back to square one, out of contact with London and useless to everyone. From that day on until the end of the Occupation I don't think I ever stopped for more than two or three hours. If I wasn't walking or riding a bicycle, or fighting, or being chased by the Germans, or the Vichyites, it just wasn't a normal day.

Fortunately, through contacts I learnt of the whereabouts

of a Free French radio operator living just over the adjacent mountain. It was hoped that he would co-operate if I mentioned the name of our mutual acquaintance. Someone lent me a man's bicycle which I half pushed and carried up the mountain but literally flew down the other side. The bike was getting up such speed that the brakes were useless, and I fell off several times. I pedalled about twenty kilometres only to find that because of all the German activity in the region, the Frenchman had left the day before. The mountain lying between me and Saint-Santin did little to lift the disappointment I felt.

Denden knew there was an SOE radio operator in Châteauroux because that is where he had spent his idyllic week while we were waiting for him in the Auvergne. He gave me as much information as he could remember and it was decided I would leave as soon as I could make myself presentable, even though it was 200 kilometres away.

We had been given the address of a friendly tailor in Aurillac but I had to wash and mend my slacks and blouse before I could appear anywhere without raising suspicion. Just then Laurent drove up in a car of all things; he had driven right around the Germans without any trouble. We were so happy to see him but livid when we thought of his comfortable trip, whereas we were all exhausted.

Laurent wouldn't give me a car to drive to Châteauroux as he said that since our battle the Germans had tightened up all regulations, and road-blocks had been installed all over the entire region. Furthermore any identity cards issued in the Cantal were suspect and by law had to be exchanged at the local police stations under the supervision of the Germans. As my identity card was from the Cantal I would have to travel without any papers. Added to which he doubted that I would get to Châteauroux on a bicycle, let alone return, and he strongly counselled Hubert to prevent me from continuing with my plan. Laurent thought that quite apart from the problems with identity cards, papers and tighter regulations, 200 kilometres was just too far to cycle. But, as I pointed out, we were useless without our radio, and this was our only immediate hope.

Once Laurent accepted the fact that I would make the trip

irrespective of all the obstacles he put in my way, he lost no time in doing everything he could to make my journey less dangerous. Men were sent in all directions to collect local information about German movements and then when he had studied all the details he mapped out the route he advised me to take. I would have to cycle about 200 kilometres of the roundabout route, without an identity card or a licence for the beautiful new ladies' bicycle a Maquisard had been able to purchase for me 'under the counter'. If I reached Châteauroux safely I would have to return by the best way I could.

While all these preparations were going on I was busy trying to get my wardrobe together. I needed an entire new outfit plus some walking shoes. I cycled into Aurillac where the tailor agreed to make me a costume in twenty-four hours, with one fitting in two hours' time. He also gave me the name and address of a cobbler who could supply me with shoes without a coupon. When I arrived at the cobbler's shop I was dismayed to hear the tailor had phoned to warn me not to return for the fitting as the Milice who were next door to his shop had already been enquiring about the woman in slacks.

The Germans had, meantime, placed road-blocks on all the main roads leading into town. I escaped by crossing several fields and heading north between two main roads until I could cross one of them and regain Saint-Santin, which lay to the west. All the way back I had been trying to think of a way to go back for my fitting. I had to find a disguise. But what? Then I had an idea.

The parents of the handsome young man in whose house we were hiding lived in the village. I went to see them and asked if they had any old clothes I could borrow. His grandmother had an old trunk with an amazing array. I borrowed a long white piqué dress which must have been fashionable before World War I. They introduced me to a farmer who was taking his horse and cart to the market in Aurillac early the next morning. I became secretive about my plans as I knew Hubert, and Denden in particular, would rag me if they saw me in my disguise. I crept out of the house early and waited for the farmer. Unfortunately, just as I had installed myself in the front of the cart beside the farmer with a pair of his trousers on my lap, which was my reason for the visit to the tailor, Denden appeared and alerted everyone else. Of course they had a good hearty laugh at my expense. Who wouldn't? There I was sitting up in the cart surrounded by fruit and vegetables looking like a real country bumpkin, wet hair pulled back tight, no make-up, an old-fashioned dress, and wearing a pair of the farmer's old boots.

Our cart and the produce were inspected several times by the Germans as we entered Aurillac; they did not give me a second look, even their first glance was rather disdainful. I did not blame them. I did not look very fetching. The only thing that boosted my morale that day was when the tailor failed to recognise me as I entered his shop. My costume was delivered the following day, and I set off for Châteauroux the day after.

On the eve of my departure Laurent sent several men on ahead to warn as many villages as they could in the Cantal and the Puy-de-Dôme to look out for me and to warn me if trouble lay ahead. In the Allier he had not been able to make any contacts so I just had to trust to luck. I had company as far as Montluçon. A Maquisard was going to visit his wife, who was ill. When we had to take the National Route we pushed our bikes instead of riding them in case any Germans approached, in which event we would have time to dive into the culverts by the side of the road until they passed.

I by-passed Montluçon and was heading for Saint-Amand. It was getting dark and I wanted to make a few enquiries. I went into a bistro and had a simple meal and a glass of wine. Listening to the conversation of the other customers, I gathered that the Germans in the area were quiet for the time being. I found a barn not far away, removed my costume and slept until the sound of an air raid awakened me.

At Saint-Amand I stopped for a coffee and overheard that Bourges had been raided the day before. When I arrived there I thought the place was quiet—not a soul in the streets and all the shutters were closed. It was only afterwards I found out that the Germans had shot some hostages that morning. I passed two groups of Germans but they made no attempt to stop me.

At Issoudon I stopped for a black-market meal, cleaned myself up and entered into conversation with the owner of the restaurant, who shared some of my wine and brandy. The dangerous part was yet to come and I needed all the local information I could obtain. There is nothing like brandy to loosen the tongue! I cycled to the local markets and filled my string bag with all the fruit and vegetables I could buy without food coupons, hoping that I would pass for a housewife out shopping. I was still making good time although my legs were beginning to ache because of the mountainous terrain I had crossed. I had cycled 200 kilometres.

There were continuous streams of German vehicles leaving Issoudon for Châteauroux so I cycled west to Brion then south-west to Villedieu-sur-Indre, and entered the city without any trouble. One German patrol was checking on the opposite side of the road but they waved me on when they saw me hesitate. I pedalled round and round the town and was just about to give in, with much despair, when I came across the bistro I was looking for. It was exactly as Denden had described it. But when I called at the SOE house they refused to help me; they refused to send a message to London. Actually their performance was completely stupid because if I had been a German or one of their agents, they would have been arrested on the spot. I left the house in disgust and returned to the bistro.

They must have been saying prayers for me back in the Auvergne because as I was pedalling around Châteauroux I had run into a Maquisard I had met several weeks before in the Corrèze. He was looking for a Free French radio operator as their operator had been killed in action. We had both agreed to help each other if one of us found our contacts and I had left him at the bistro where he was waiting when I returned with the bad news.

Off we pedalled to find his contact, who was also a patron of a bistro which was situated opposite the home of the radio operator. He warned us that the Germans had not caught the radio operator but they were in the house waiting to trap any callers.

The town was literally swarming with Germans. They were completely surrounding areas and checking the houses systematically, so we decided to leave immediately. We separated and arranged to meet outside the town. Both of us were able to by-pass the road-blocks and, wasting no time, we

134

headed for a Maquis group my companion knew in the Creuse. The leader belonged to the Free French and had come from Algiers, where his headquarters were. He was understanding when I told him the trouble I was in and said that if his radio operator did not object to sending my message, neither would he. The operator agreed to my request to send a message to Colonel Buckmaster in London via the Free French in Algiers. I wished my travelling companion good luck and was on my way.

By now I was so tired I resolved to take the quickest route home. Every kilometre I pedalled was sheer agony. I knew that if I ever got off the bike, I could never get on it again, so I kept pedalling. Halfway across the Allier the companion I had left in Montluçon was looking out for me. He had guessed the road I would take if all went well. His wife had presented him with a baby son and they were both well, so he was happy. I arrived back in Saint-Santin twenty-four hours before the time they had anticipated I would, even though they were well aware I might never return. I had pedalled 500 kilometres in seventy-two hours.

They greeted me with open arms and shouts of joy. All I could do was cry. When I got off that damned bike I felt as if I had a fire between my legs and the inside of my thighs were raw. I couldn't stand up, I couldn't sit down, I couldn't walk and I didn't sleep for days. But thanks to all the help I had been given by one and all, I had succeeded and all we had to do now was to wait and see if Algiers sent our signal on to Colonel Buckmaster. They did. As I said to Hubert, Denden and Bazooka, I never wanted to be told any more that the Free French agents in the field would not help the British ones, because I knew better. I never heard of that group in the Creuse after that so I have never been able to say 'thank you' in peacetime.

It took me a few days to recover. The doctor from the village had dressed my thighs which were in a horrible state but there was little else anyone could do. My three close colleagues looked in frequently to see how I was faring, but I just wanted to be left alone. When I'm asked what I'm most proud of doing during the war, I say 'the bike ride'.

Finally the day came when I could move without experiencing too much pain, and I dressed and went out to lunch. To my surprise a strange Frenchman, to whom I was not introduced, was sitting at my table. He had arrived during my absence, stating that he was a full Colonel in the regular French Army and that he was going to take over our outfit and run it on correct military lines. Hubert had not been game to tell me that this man had been our uninvited guest for days.

Normally one could ask for identity papers but in those days it was pointless to do so as everybody's papers in the Resistance were false. Perhaps he was a Colonel. I neither knew or cared. All I could see was that now victory was so close too many people wanted to jump on the bandwagon and play that ugly game of politics. I had been a budding journalist in the thirties and witnessed the havoc caused by politicians and other power-hungry individuals, so I was not impressed by this 'Colonel's' speech.

When he had finished his pep-talk, obviously for my ears as the others had heard it before, I asked him what he was going to do for money and arms, because I certainly was not going to give him any of ours. Hubert looked embarrassed but Bazooka, Denden and the rest of our group did not try to conceal their joy. The four of us discussed this new situation later and they agreed with my suggestion that we all move further north towards Tardivat, the gallant Frenchman who greeted me when I dropped into France. Tardivat was not a politician. From then on until the end of the Occupation we never looked back.

When Hubert and I drove up north to the *département* of the Allier and towards Tardivat, Bazooka was left in charge, with Denden detailed to listen to all the BBC personal messages in the event we received a signal from London acknowledging our SOS and perhaps confirming the parachutage we requested.

Tardivat was delighted to see us. Immediately he found a suitable site for our group not far from Ygrande and near a field we had been using for air-drops. Hubert remained with him to prepare the camp, while I returned to Saint-Santin to fetch our belongings and the men, who were 200 strong.

Not only did I find London had received our signal, they had already sent me my own radio operator, who would share his codes with Denden. Roger was a good-looking American Marine, aged nineteen. He spoke very little French but they all liked him and he fitted into our life-style smoothly. Unhappily for us all, Bazooka had been ordered to the Clermont–Ferrand area to instruct another Maquis group.

Hubert had been working hard setting up our camp and we all settled in straightaway. The men were still part of the Maquis d'Auvergne but they were more or less our own special group attached to our Allied team. We were lucky to have them with us; they were all good men, we knew them personally and, like the Americans and British, they had no political aspirations. They only wanted to get rid of the enemy and return to their families. That night we were joined by thirty young Frenchmen, all evaders from the *relève*—the German compulsory labour force. They were enthusiastic but as yet untrained.

I was heartily sick of sleeping on the damp ground and when one day Tarvidat asked me for an extra quantity of Bren guns which were in short supply, I bribed him by promising Brens for a bus. However, I stipulated a bus with two long seats in the rear, facing each other, so I could balance the big mattress (also procured by Tardivat) on top of them. He took a few men down to a main road and set up a road-block. As each bus reached the barriers he made all the passengers alight while he inspected the rear. This procedure continued until a suitable bus arrived. The poor passengers must have been petrified by the sight of the Maquisards, all armed to the teeth and looking fierce. The passengers in the unsuitable buses must have been mystified also when they were allowed to continue their journey. Naturally he received his Bren guns. He was going to get them anyway. So I used to sleep in the back of the bus, on a beautiful soft mattress with nylon parachutes for sheets, and entertain in the front.

Somehow or other I'd managed to have with me a couple of pretty nighties, leftovers from another life. No matter how tired I was, after a day in a male world, wearing trousers, I'd change into a frilly nightie to sleep in my bus.

Our immediate plan at Ygrande was to increase the level of security which had been impossible when we were attached to the oversized groups further south. We had a conference with our men and it was decided unanimously that we would never remain in one spot more than three or four days. If the site happened to be in a particularly favourable position we could stay one week, but no longer. As soon as we moved to one place we would agree on the next one and the leaders would be informed. In the case of a sudden attack my bus would be loaded immediately with wireless equipment, the operators themselves and my bicycle, and proceed to our rendezvous point. A driver and one man were detailed to enforce this rule.

We had not been in Ygrande two days when our lookouts warned us that a large body of Germans were approaching. Our withdrawal went like clockwork. Three thousand Huns wasted all their ammunition to capture one empty farmhouse. We were all delighted, as can well be imagined.

Two American weapons instructors were to be dropped at a field nearby that same night. Remembering the complete lack of security when I had been introduced to the entire village of Cosne-d'Allier, I determined that things would be different when these two arrived. And they were different, almost unique, in fact.

They arrived safely, although one of them had lost his suitcase and we took them straight back to our camp, where we entertained them in the bus. Naturally we greeted these two Americans, John Alsop and Reeve Schley, with French champagne. They did not speak much French but we didn't mind as long as they could instruct the Maquis groups in the use of our weapons. They gave us news from London and we carried on talking and drinking until about four in the morning.

They looked smart in their uniforms, especially Schley who had on beautiful leather cavalry boots. I knew that when our men saw how well dressed they were they would start moaning again about our uniforms. All we could give them were socks, boots, khaki trousers and shirts, and they were dying to have decent uniforms. We took them to their simple quarters which Denden and I had cleaned up; we had even put some wildflowers in a jamjar next to their beds. As we left, one of them asked quite casually if we ever got attacked, and quite casually I replied that we had just been attacked the day before but I didn't think the Germans would be back that day. That

138

proved to be the understatement of the year. They were already at our back door.

I woke up when the Germans started firing and yelled out to the Americans who were close by to get up—we were being attacked. We couldn't find Hubert; he had disappeared. As we learnt much later, he had got up early to find the missing suitcase before anyone else did. Schley must have been in such a hurry to get dressed that he put on his cavalry boots first and couldn't get his trousers on, so reckoning he didn't have time to start all over again, he cut his trousers with a knife and appeared in front of me in short scalloped trousers. I wasn't much better—I hadn't time to take my pink satin nightdress off and it was showing under my shirt.

Our 200 men had disappeared to fight and our 'High Command', consisting only of Denden and me, were packing everything into my bus which had started to leave when I noticed the bicycle was left behind. Denden raced over and threw it on top of the bus, and immediately started screaming blue murder. He had got caught on some electric wires! Roger and the driver were laughing their heads off. I was doubled up, tears running down my face. All this time the Americans were standing there surveying the scene amidst the sound of machine-gun fire, grenades and what have you.

Thank goodness they didn't understand much French, as the scouts soon came back with the news that we were being attacked by 6,000 Germans. We were 200 plus two in the High Command, two newly arrived Americans and thirty new recruits. We were definitely outnumbered. For a while we hoped Hubert would arrive with some reinforcements, but he was trapped, kilometres away.

Then some of our defenders came back and said the Germans were well entrenched but why couldn't we try the bazookas that had been dropped the previous night and which they were obviously dying to try out. The problem was that the two instructors were the only ones who knew how to use them, and they couldn't speak French. But our men insisted they could knock out a few German posts if only someone would show them what to do. Those poor Americans! It was like a scene from a comic opera.

The wounded were being brought in so I put the other

member of the High Command, Denden, in charge of them, irrespective of his plea that he didn't like the sight of blood. I gave him plenty of bandages and a gallon of pure alcohol. I didn't issue him with any arms as he didn't like them either.

We collected all the bazookas and prepared to face the enemy, the two non-French-speaking instructors, the interpreter (me), and two men for each bazooka. I think our new recruits must have thought it was going to be a piece of cake because twenty of them volunteered to carry some of our material. I warned them to stick to the woods but they unfortunately disobeyed my orders and took a short-cut. Seven of them were killed immediately by the German machine-guns. The other thirteen fled back to our camp.

The rest of us carried on regardless. Everything was put in place, the Americans instructed on bazookas, firing of. I ran from one crew to another translating. They knocked out several German posts and when we had exhausted our supply of ammunition (some had not been unpacked) we withdrew. This may have been a first for the Americans but it was also a first for me. I had never been on a battlefield translating from English into French on how to fire a bazooka.

We returned to our camp to find Denden with a loaded carbine slung over his shoulder, a row of grenades fastened on to his belt, and a Colt. The man who was afraid of guns! He was also very, very drunk. He had been drinking the pure alcohol as he tended the wounded, and it had given him Dutch courage. I removed the grenades as he could have not only killed himself, he could have killed us too, and I had enough trouble on my plate.

I kept my fingers crossed as I told Alsop and Schley that everything would be all right and asked one of our scouts to show me the way to the Spaniards' camp. We crawled across several fields and when I reached one of their outposts I asked the sentry on duty to ask his Colonel to send my SOS to Tardivat.

When I returned to our camp Schley said he didn't want the Germans to smoke the Havana cigars his father had given him back in New York, so the three of us sat down and puffed away as if we didn't have a care in the world. Suddenly we heard the sound of Bren guns and mortars to the rear of the

Germans. I yelled out to everyone: 'Tardivat, let's go!' He gave us time to retreat, then retreated himself, leaving the Germans to conquer a deserted campsite.

Tardivat and his men had been sitting down to lunch when he received my SOS. I was amazed that Frenchmen would leave their meal, and said so flippantly. All he said was, 'Aren't you glad you gave me all those Bren guns?' However, he had saved our lives. We had smoked those cigars for nothing! All this happened during the first twelve hours after the Americans' arrival, and I had planned such a pleasant and relaxed day for them, a day they would remember. They would certainly remember it, but for entirely different reasons.

We found Hubert hiding in a barn. Having retrieved Schley's suitcase he had been cut off from us when the fighting had begun and had therefore been unable to assist in any way.

Several of our badly wounded men were smuggled into a private hospital run by a religious order. The seven reckless young men who had died so tragically were laid to rest in a nearby cemetery. They were buried with all the military honours possible considering the danger of conducting such a service.

We stayed near the Spanish camp for a couple of days and moved onto a good site in the Forêt de Tronçais. It was well concealed, protected by Tardivat's groups and, to our delight, near a large pond where we were able to enjoy the pleasure of bathing ourselves, instead of having to carry out our ablutions from a small bucket of water. If we were bathing during the daytime we either dived under the water or made a dash for the forest when German planes flew overhead.

We were receiving new recruits every day. Alsop and Schley were kept busy all day long instructing them on the use of weapons and explosives, fortunately within the peace of our forest and not on the battlefield!

The Americans had brought their cameras with them and they had, unknown to me, taken a snap of me getting out of my pink satin nightdress. Denden had told them of my famous satin nightdresses, one pink and one blue. However mannish I looked by day, I always slept in satin.

I determined to get even. I waited until Schley went to bathe one morning. He undressed and left his clothes and camera by a tree. I took the camera and sat by the water's edge, waiting for him to emerge. After being in the icy cold water for thirty minutes he was blue in the face but he would not admit defeat. The German planes appeared on the horizon and he was forced to reassess his predicament. We always found time to play jokes on one another and enjoy a good laugh. It became a battle of wits between the sexes.

There had been nothing violent about my nature before the war yet the years would see a great change. But in spite of my virulent attitude to the enemy I could not condone torture and brutality on our part, although I was not foolish enough to believe they would extend me the same courtesy. Consequently the day I was informed confidentially by a man in our Maquis that a group nearby were holding three females, one of whom was a German spy, I threatened to disarm them if they did not release the poor unfortunate women into my custody. All three had been ill-treated and used as if they were prostitutes.

The leader of the group concerned was a married man. I had accepted his hospitality before he had joined the Maquis. When I learnt his wife had been aware of the brutality meted out to the women I was horrified to think I had been friendly with them both.

The two French girls were no problem, but the German girl could not be set free. I interrogated her and she admitted she had been sent to spy on the Maquis and then to report back to the Gestapo. She hated the French and the British as much as I hated her people. Reluctantly I informed her she would have to be shot as there was no alternative under the circumstances.

At first the men refused to shoot a woman and agreed to form a firing squad only after I had announced I would undertake the task myself. She spat at me as she passed and shouted 'Heil Hitler' before she died.

For my part I showed absolutely no emotion as she walked to her death. How had this been possible? How had I become so aggressive? It was simple. I remembered Vienna, Berlin and the Jews. I remembered seeing a poor French woman, seven months pregnant, tied to a stake and bayonetted, criss-cross, in the stomach by a German soldier. Her screaming two-year-old held her hand and she was left to die with her unborn child. A German officer stood by and watched the soldier carry out his orders. I remembered my friend in the escape-route network who was beheaded with an axe after he had been captured by the Gestapo. The enemy had made me tough. I had no pity for them nor would I expect any in return.

I have returned to Germany many times since their defeat. They have worked hard to rebuild their Fatherland. It is a lovely country to visit and although I am quite happy to be friendly with some young Germans I keep well away from the older generation in case I become involved with some ex-Nazi. I will never be able to forget the misery and death they caused to so many millions of innocent people; the savage brutality, the sadism, the unnecessary bloodshed, the slaughter and inhuman acts they performed on other human beings. I am inclined to feel sorry for the young Germans of today, knowing how utterly miserable I would be if I was descended from a Nazi.

War is a calamity. It is destructive and brings great sorrow and loss of life. But at least it is, or should be, a clear-cut manoeuvre between two opposing nations fighting each other until one side admits defeat. Civil war is disastrous because it means two or more parts of a nation fighting for supremacy. Although I did not go to Spain during the Civil War I was always in close touch with people who did.

By July 1944 there were so many branches of the Resistance it was difficult to keep track of them. There were right-wingers, left-wingers, red-hot Communists, government officials, civil servants, ex-Vichyites, ex-Milicians, secret army, regular army and dozens more, besides masses of individuals trying to get on the bandwagon. We kept our distance from the would-be politicians, concentrating on arming the Maquisards as efficiently and rapidly as possible.

Hubert was fully occupied with the leaders of the adjacent groups, discussing and executing plans that would frustrate the Germans wherever and whenever the opportunity arose. They attacked the enemy convoys on the road, they intercepted and stole hundreds of wagon-loads of food being transported to Germany, they set up ambushes in the most unlikely places and generally made the existence of the Germans in the area a perilous one. Apart from these activities they manned the dropping zones at night and in their spare time they prepared the explosives needed to destroy the targets we had been assigned.

Laurent had provided me with a new car and a driver who knew the Allier and the Puy-de-Dôme like the back of his hand. I would contact dozens and dozens of groups of men hiding in forests. After meeting their leaders I would assess their groups, most of whom impressed me, and would promise to arm their men and also contribute a certain amount of money towards their subsistence.

Sometimes Roger accompanied me. He was not as good or experienced an operator as Denden but he was more relaxed and never complained about the conditions under which he worked. If he had to transmit or receive messages while we were travelling by car we would pull into the side of the road, he would throw the aerial over a tree, sit on the wheel or bumper bar, balance his set on his knee and tap away in Morse code. If we ran out of distilled water he never made a fuss like Denden did, he would simply substitute ordinary water.

I had to find new fields where we could organise our air-drops. This was becoming more and more difficult as the Germans were attacking Maquis groups every day in retaliation. Roger and I had to shoot our way out of a road-block on two occasions and we were extremely fortunate to escape capture.

One day I was obliged to go to Vichy. When my business there was concluded I decided to treat myself to a good meal in an expensive black-market restaurant before returning to the forest. A member of an unruly group of men (whom, incidentally, I had refused to arm) had apparently been informed of my extravagance and decided I had been spending money to which his so-called 'Resistance' group was entitled. He was quite wrong as Hubert, Denden and I always received our own personal allowances from London. This ignorant and uncouth individual was airing his views about our British team in a café in a little village where I was due at midday. My visit had obviously been discussed there. He became very, very inebriated and announced he was going to kill me. He then opened a case and displayed several grenades. The patron of the café became alarmed and was going to dispatch someone to warn me as soon as I arrived on the outskirts of the village.

This village was old, with narrow streets. The only way a motorist could drive through it was to take a blind alleyway where a reflecting mirror warned of the traffic ahead. The café was only a few metres away.

I was early, and blissfully unaware of the drama about to unfold. When the would-be assassin heard a car approaching he took a grenade out of the case, removed the pin and held it in his hand. When he saw a woman in the car he went to throw it but he was so drunk he had forgotten the pin was out and it blew up in his hand. I saw the explosion and bits of human flesh all over the place, but it was a few minutes before I heard the story. I could not feel sorry for him. He and his men were the types who pretended to be members of the Resistance and at times gave it a bad name.

This story reached the forest via 'bush wireless' before I returned. It was decided there and then that I would have a bodyguard whenever I travelled by car. Tardivat suggested we approach the Spanish group and their colonel immediately delegated six of his best men to protect me.

We must have made an impressive sight as our three cars sped along the roads. They had installed a Bren machine-gun in the windscreen of each car and another one at the rear. Whenever possible we remained on the secondary roads, which were covered in red dust. As I always travelled in the second car I arrived at our destination looking like a Red Indian, so after the first trip I transferred to the first car. I tried to explain in Spanish that it was because of vanity and not bravery but I don't think it convinced them.

These six Spaniards became devoted to me and I never had any worries when I was with them, even though at times we were obliged to use the National Routes. If we stopped at a village for a meal and anyone dared to look sideways at me they would stand there looking fierce with their Sten guns at the ready. They would inspect the kitchens and one day they forced two men to show their identity cards simply because they were staring at me during lunch. They were experienced fighters, having gone through the Spanish Civil War. I must have covered thousands of kilometres with my bodyguard. To me it was all very theatrical but the Spaniards took it seriously. I often wondered what the people thought of our little convoy as we passed through the villages.

In the latter part of July and during August I was travelling continuously. Every night hundreds of containers filled with weapons and explosives were being parachuted on to our fields in anticipation of the Allied landings, which ultimately took place in the south of France on 15 August.

The arrival of the Americans—especially as they were officers wearing such splendid uniforms—had boosted the morale of the Maquisards in the area to such an extent that we had intended to hold a banquet in their honour. The battle the morning after their arrival and several subsequent mishaps had forced us to abandon all major social activities. However, as Tardivat pointed out, we now had two important events to celebrate: firstly, the arrival of our American instructors and secondly, my lucky escape. We chose a night when the moon was low as we would be unlikely to receive an air-drop.

Tardivat was in charge of all the catering arrangements. He conferred with a chef in a nearby town who prepared most of the food in his hotel. The morning of the banquet he was 'kidnapped' at gun-point and taken to our forest. The alleged kidnapping was to protect him in case he was interrogated by the Germans or the Milicians at a later date.

Denden, assisted by several experts, installed an elaborate row of lights overhead which could be turned off immediately if our sentries warned us of enemy planes approaching. Our tables consisted of long logs covered by white sheets borrowed from friendly villagers. The chef served a magnificent eight-course meal, accompanied by some superb French wines. He hovered around looking impressive wearing his snow-white chef's hat and apron, assisted by several volunteers from our group, suitably dressed for the occasion.

It was a banquet I will never forget, and most certainly one that could never be repeated. Several hundred men attended and every single one had been spending hours trying to make his clothes look as smart as possible. The lighting system was a huge success—our part of the forest looked like a fairyland. Tardivat greeted the guests with typical French formality and the foreign guests responded with great dignity! We toasted everyone and everything. We swore our eternal allegiance and love to France, Great Britain and the United States of America. When we couldn't think of anything else to toast we swayed to our feet and toasted the Germans and the Allied Forces for not having interrupted our gala dinner.

Half-way through this extraordinary banquet a serious French Maquisard was escorted to my table by a sentry. He was delivering a message from his leader. Naturally we invited him to join our party. He looked at all the food on the tables and the piles of empty bottles on the ground and the full ones in the process of being consumed, and asked me if this was the style in which we dined every night. We managed to keep a serious face and everyone who had heard his question replied, 'Yes, of course, don't you?'

In the early hours of the morning a violent thunder and lightning storm forced us to scurry back to our respective camps in a disorderly fashion. The bright and almost continuous flashes of lightning made it easy for me to find my way to my bus, but the ground had become like a bog and I was soaking wet and covered with mud by the time I reached it. Furthermore, I was feeling sorry for myself and for the unceremonious manner in which our banquet had been terminated.

Soon after installing ourselves in the forest we had bought a horse, especially for Roger as sometimes he got bored, although Schley exercised it if he had the time. As I was trying to clean my clothes I heard the horse neighing. I looked through the window and there he was in the pouring rain making a terrible noise. Immediately I stopped feeling sorry for myself and proceeded to lavish all my love and sympathy on the poor unfortunate horse. We had a galvanised iron lean-to attached to my bus which we used as a makeshift bathroom and where we kept all our toilet necessities. I dragged the horse in, talking to him all the time, telling him not to worry about the storm as I would look after him. Then I fell asleep.

I woke up several hours later. The horse and the galvanised-iron roof had disappeared. Actually he was foolish to run away as, with the meat shortage, he could not have gone far before ending up in some hungry person's saucepan. We found the roof some distance away. The contents of our bathroom were ruined as they were all mixed up with horse manure. Alsop had been sleeping under a yellow parachute. The rain had soaked through it, so he appeared looking as if he had jaundice. Denden took one look at him and went back to bed. That night our personal message to the BBC was 'Andrée had a horse in the bathroom'.

Thank goodness the Germans did not attack that night.

Without doubt, Tardivat was the man I most admired then. He was intelligent, disciplined, reliable, honest and very brave. He also had a fantastic sense of fun, which I appreciated. When I was not on the road he would invite me to take part in some of his escapades. We carried out several ambushes together and blew up a few small bridges. If any German convoys were foolish enough to pass through his area he always managed to do some damage to their vehicles. In suitable terrain we loved using what we called a 'trip wire'. It was attached to a tree on each side of the road and the first vehicle in the convoy would blow up. We liked to be concealed on a nearby hill so we could watch the confusion before withdrawing to a safer spot.

The most exciting sortie I ever made with Tardivat was an attack on the German headquarters in Montluçon. He and his men organised this raid from beginning to end. All the weapons and explosives used were hidden in a house near the headquarters, ready to be picked up just after noon when the Germans would be enjoying their pre-lunch drinks. Each one of us had received specific orders. I entered the building by the back door, raced up the stairs, opened the first door along the passage way and threw in my grenades, closed the door and ran like hell back to my car which was ready to make a quick getaway. The headquarters was completely wrecked inside the building, and several dozen Germans did not lunch that day, nor any other day for that matter. The hardest part of the raid was to convince the nearby residents that the Allies had not landed and that they should return immediately to their homes and remain indoors.

In the early hours of the morning of 15 August, the long-awaited invasion of the south of France became a reality. Nearly 300,000 troops, comprised of Americans, British, Canadians and French, disembarked between Toulon and

Cannes. The Resistance movements all over France had been anxiously awaiting the landings, as it would mean the beginning of the end for the Germans.

The numerous Maquis groups in the Allier set about destroying the targets they had been assigned for the second D-day. I'd brought the plans for these raids from England in that handbag—the bridges, roads, cable lines, railways, factories—anything that could be of use to the Germans. They destroyed them all except one which was a synthetic petrol plant at Saint-Hilaire. Tardivat, who had seized the entire output of fuel two months previously, said it would be a shame to destroy the plant as another supply of fuel would soon be available. London gave us permission to leave the plant intact as long as we could be certain the fuel would not fall into German hands.

Tardivat, plus the Anglo-American team, backed by several of our most bloodthirsty-looking Maquisards, called to see the plant manager at his home. He was not a bit co-operative when we informed him we were going to run his plant for the Allies. However, he was taken by force to the distillery and then to the boardroom, where he was interrogated by the male members of our team. He was warned that his failure to comply with their orders would have drastic consequences and that as he had traded with the enemy he would be put under arrest and placed under the charge of the Maquis.

He was white in the face and trembling by this time and assured us he would reserve the total output of fuel for the Maquis, mentioning the amount we could expect. I had not been included in this particular conversation, I was just standing by, armed to the teeth and trying to look as fierce as possible. Nevertheless, I did not want to be left out of the proceedings so I piped up and said that according to the figures I had, the amount of fuel he promised was not the entire output. To everyone's surprise, including my own, he agreed that perhaps it could be a little more. Tardivat left several men to protect our interests and keep an eye on the manager, but he was so scared of the Maquis he did not put a foot wrong after that day. Now we were all oil kings we made for the nearest bistro to celebrate our success.

All our operations were not as comical as our Saint-Hilaire

one had been, but as the weeks sped by and the Germans were on the run, both from the Allied Forces and the French Resistance, it was often possible to enjoy a little light relief as we carried on with our duties.

At long last the Germans were paying a high price for the suffering they had inflicted on the French people. They knew the Resistance was lurking everywhere, just waiting to pounce. Too often the enemy had behaved like savages and now they were afraid for their own lives.

We trooped over to Cosne-d'Allier, the little village where Hubert and I had stayed when we first arrived. As we had been introduced to the entire village, they all came out of their houses when they saw me and followed us around when we laid our charges on the bridges and road junctions. It was the most enthusiastic audience we had ever seen or heard. They jumped up and down as each was detonated, and clapped and cheered as we withdrew. The difficult part of the operation had been to keep the villagers at a safe distance.

Tardivat decided, after his success with the German headquarters, that he would like to attack their garrison at Montluçon, where the force had been reduced to about 3,000. He set off with about 300 men and Alsop, Schley and Hubert. All the leaders were armed with bazookas—a popular weapon during World War II and especially suitable for the Maquis. Alsop and Schley led their groups while Hubert returned to our camp with a message from Tardivat inviting me to join in the fun. I had just finished coding my signals for London so I grabbed a bazooka, my carbine and several grenades, and set off for Montluçon in Hubert's car. When we reached the town and made enquiries as to Tardivat's position we were informed that he had captured half the garrison and we would have to cross a certain bridge in order to reach him. The only trouble was that as we began crossing the bridge someone opened fire with machine-guns. I got out of the car and started waving to Tardivat up in the garrison. It wasn't Tardivat, it was a German, and we were on the wrong bridge. We did a quick about-turn but the others teased us for days.

The fort was held for several days but the Germans sent over strong reinforcements from the east and the Maquis withdrew back to the forest. However, the whole town and

150

Maquisards in the grounds of the château attempting to train some gendarmes who joined their group.

(From left) *Colonel Paishing, leader of the Spanish Maquis contingent; Roger, the radio operator (in white shirt); and two of Nancy's Spanish bodyguards* (right and foreground).

(Left and below) *On the steps of the château on Nancy's birthday in August 1944, waiting for the Maquis to present arms. Nancy is in front.*

Saluting while the Maquis march past.

(Above and below) *Retreating Germans on the main road near the château in July or August 1944, photographed by an American hidden in bushes.*

(Above left)
Nancy at the Lido cabaret in Paris in 1946.

(Above right)
Nancy during her trip to California, aged about 60.

Nancy with her husband, John Forward.

Back in France, 1984, at the cemetery where the Maquis buried their dead.

the temporary victors could not conceal the satisfaction the event had given them.

It had rained for days, and the forest was like a quagmire. We were soaked to the skin and thoroughly miserable. Now that the Germans had troubles of their own they no longer presented a great threat to the Maquis and we determined to find more comfortable quarters. We were told of Fragne, an empty château a few kilometres from Montluçon. The owner had inherited it from an aunt but as he had not been able to install electricity and running water it had never attracted the attention of the Germans. Hubert and I talked to the caretaker, and through her the owner gave us permission to occupy the château for as long as we wished.

It was a huge place with spacious rooms. We slept on mattresses or in sleeping-bags and it was absolute bliss to be out of the rain. There was a lovely old clock-tower and a deep well at the rear of the château where we fetched our water for washing purposes, but for cooking the caretaker allowed us to fill our buckets from her kitchen tap. We moved in about one week before my birthday, which was on 30 August. As the men were all walking around looking secretive I guessed they were planning some kind of celebration.

We were occupied day and night. Alsop and Schley were instructing men on the use of the weapons and explosives we were receiving; Hubert was conferring with the other leaders; and I was receiving air-drops every night of the moon period. I had about twenty fields scattered all over the area but I decided that in future we would use the grounds of the château for any air-drops intended for our own use.

The men laughed when I announced this but realising I was serious they immediately volunteered to assist me to try to make the plan functional. They prepared an elaborate lighting system, using every available battery, and after a trial run we were convinced we could retire to our beds if the planes were delayed or cancelled. Should we hear them coming while we were in bed, we could switch on the lights which were already in position, hop out of bed and be on the field in time for the reception. London was informed immediately of our latest dropping zone.

At the headquarters of the Special Operations Executive, a

Canadian ready to be parachuted on our new field found the château was marked on the Michelin map and wanted to know what idiot was using it. They informed him. Apparently all he said was, 'Oh, Nancy.' He was the chap who blew up the condom at Beaulieu. He and his travelling companions dropped quite safely on our field. We ushered them into our château with great pride and extended our usual hospitality.

Paris was liberated on 25 August 1944, and the whole country rejoiced; it would be hard to describe the excitement in the air. After defeat and years of humiliation their beautiful capital was free. The aggressors were now the hunted. The Germans were on the run and the French people were overcome with joy. My men were organising a surprise for my birthday and at the same time we were going to celebrate the Liberation of Paris.

It was a wonderful party, which happily the Germans did not interrupt. All our colleagues were invited and so was our landlord. If anyone was unable to attend the luncheon, they came along afterwards. Everyone we knew helped us obtain the food and wine. It was amazing to see how many bottles of wine and champagne some farmers had been able to bury in their fields. Madame Renard and her daughter were guests. We supplied the ingredients for the marvellous dessert tarts and cakes she made for our party.

When all the guests had arrived we were escorted to the steps of the terrace leading into the rear entrance of the château. It was a secluded spot and could not be seen from the main road, which the Germans were still using. I was presented with a magnificent bouquet of flowers and told at the same time to be ready to take the salute. That was the surprise they had been planning. I was amazed to see we had so many smart, well-trained men. There were hundreds and hundreds of them. Then suddenly I recognised a man I had already seen marching by. The penny dropped. Once they had marched past our steps they ran like the devil right around the château and rejoined the men ahead. Without doubt they were the finest and fittest body of fighters I have ever had the honour and privilege to salute.

We gathered in the immense hall where rows of makeshift tables had been erected. Beautiful floral decorations surrounded the tables so that the emptiness of the vast room was not noticed. The speeches were endless and became more and more sentimental as we consumed bottle after bottle of the best wines and champagne France could offer.

There was only one sad note. Madame Renard's daughter announced at the table that Alex, Denden's boyfriend, had been killed. She had not known of the relationship between the two. We had to console him the best way we could but I'm afraid we were all too busy to be able to sympathise with appropriate dignity.

Everyone brought me some little gift. They must have been searching in the villages for ages as at that time everything was in short supply. My Spaniards, who had absolutely no money, had gathered all the wildflowers they could find in the forest and wrapped them in a Spanish flag, and one of the bodyguard had written me a poem. It was all very touching. The party continued until the early hours of the morning. It was a great success and the talk of the Allier for some time.

When the Germans evacuated Montluçon, we were lucky. The château had been empty for so long and still, from the outside, looked deserted. The whole German convoy passed by without disturbing our Allied team hiding inside.

In September 1944 the Germans evacuated Vichy. Gaspard and Hubert had prearranged to join forces and enter the town at the same time. But Gaspard had stolen a march on us and gone on ahead. We gathered our team together and hurried after him. Vichy represented everything we had been fighting against, and we were determined to be a part of its liberation.

The collaborators seemed to have vanished into thin air and the crowds in the street went wild with joy. All through the night we were fêted wherever we went.

A ceremony was organised the following morning at the Cenotaph. All the assembled groups were to lay wreaths. I was nominated by our Allied team to represent them. When the mayor had finished his address, a woman emerged from the crowds and came towards me. She had been a receptionist at the Hôtel du Louvre et Paix in Marseille. Quite abruptly she informed me that Henri was dead. I was stunned. I do not know whether I had decided it was unreasonable to let the nightmare I had had in London influence my feelings; perhaps

I had subconsciously put the dream at the back of my mind and determined to carry on as if it had not happened. But I do know that ever since my return to France I had been taking it for granted that Henri was alive. I burst into tears. Denis took me away.

I wanted to go straight to Marseille to find out what had happened. Laurent, who was a magician where vehicles were concerned, put our car into perfect running order and the five of us raced down to Marseille—Hubert, Denden, John Alsop, our doctor friend Pierre Vellat and myself. It was a chaotic journey. The Allied Air Force had destroyed all the major bridges and the Resistance had sabotaged the targets they had been given for the landing in the south of France. Furthermore, everyone on the road seemed to be going north. We were the only ones going in the opposite direction. Finally, we arrived in Marseille.

I went straight to my butcher's shop, which was closed, so I went around to the back entrance and tapped on the kitchen window. They recognised me and I could see the look of alarm that passed between them as they wondered whether I was aware of the bad news. I put them at ease at once, then asked about Picon. The Ficetoles had taken him when Henri had been arrested, but their home had been destroyed in one of the air raids and no one knew if they were dead or alive.

After spending hours searching for them we were directed to a little place outside Marseille. There was no answer when I knocked on the door but Picon was inside and started howling. After twenty months he had recognised my voice. He was so excited when he was let out after the Ficetoles returned that our doctor, Pierre, had to give him tranquillisers.

Henri had been arrested by the Gestapo in May 1943. He had been imprisoned until his death on 16 October, five months later. It was in the middle of October that I had had that nightmare in London.

We returned to the château. Picon, who would not let me out of his sight, came too. We found dozens of invitations waiting there for us from all the towns and villages where we had been known.

I think that somehow I'd been subconsciously mourning Henri since the dream in London nearly a year before. Nothing was going to bring him back, and in spite of my grief I could not be unhappy knowing I'd contributed to the Liberation of France.

Our group of men at the château was preparing to go home. The Americans returned to London. We left the château in good order, thanked the landlord and caretaker for their kindness, and the three of us dawdled back to Paris. All along the route the French were celebrating the Liberation and it seemed to be one glorious party after another. We thought we might be the last ones to report back to Paris, where SOE had opened a branch, but a few more stragglers were still enjoying French hospitality.

Paris had been liberated in August 1944, but it would be another nine months of fighting across France before the German surrender in May 1945. After Paris was freed, Tardivat joined the army and kept fighting. Tragically, after all his adventures as a Maquis leader, he lost a leg in the fighting at Belfort Gap.

As there was a long waiting list for seats on an Allied Transport plane, we proceeded to enjoy ourselves in Paris. Denden spent a whole day at the hairdresser and came out looking ten years younger. Hubert disappeared for days. It transpired he had been looking after his future and organised himself an interesting position in a government department. I tried to trace old friends. Some were dead—some, including Stephanie, had disappeared and others had not returned from the country areas where they had taken refuge.

CHAPTER TEN

We returned to England on 16 October 1944. It was a terrible flight and the cabin was bitterly cold. We were sitting on the hard floor, leaning on the side of the plane. Another ten minutes in the air would have made me violently air-sick.

Five of us were travelling on the same military document issued by the British authorities in Paris. We presented ourselves to the immigration authorities only to be told that we three were not expected. I couldn't believe it. The year before Gibraltar had slipped up—surely SOE could not be guilty of such an oversight. I was all for making a fuss immediately but Hubert said we should sit down and wait patiently while the immigration officer telephoned SOE headquarters. I agreed to wait one hour and not one minute longer.

Shortly afterwards we were informed that our headquarters had never heard of us. When the hour was up I waited another fifteen minutes and then I exploded. I informed them I was going to London immediately and if they were thinking of detaining me they would be well advised to enlist the assistance of the police. By this time all the immigration officers involved were running around in circles. Denden was delighted. Hubert was just sitting there looking glum and not doing one single thing to help.

As I caught the first transport, followed closely by Denden, one of the officers asked for my address in London in case Colonel Buckmaster wished to contact me. I called out, 'Why? He doesn't know me.' At the last minute Hubert decided to brave the wrath of the immigration officers and come with us but we were so cross with him we ignored him all the way to London. The next day at our office I was not surprised to be assured by SOE that they had not received any enquiries from the immigration authorities. I will never know what possessed them to act as they did.

Some time later we were back in France, accompanying Colonel Buckmaster on a tour of the Allier and the Auvergne.

We introduced him to as many leaders as we could, and as always, the French hospitality was unsurpassable. I said good-bye to the many friends I had made in the Maquis and returned to Marseille where I guessed I would find many problems.

It was a depressing time for me, tidying up the loose ends of my marriage and attending to neglected business matters. I remained in Marseille until the German surrender in May 1945. While I was in Marseille, a padre, who had occupied the same cell as Henri, returned from a German concentration camp and went out of his way to trace me. With great sorrow I listened to the story of the last few days of Henri's life, and of how he'd been tortured.

His father had contacted one of his close friends who was also a collaborator in Marseille and enlisted his help in trying to bargain with the Gestapo. He informed his son that if he divulged my whereabouts to the Gestapo they would release him immediately. Henri told his father to leave him in peace and to be sure to look after Nancy.

Henri's doctor friend invited me to lunch one day before I left Marseille. I imagined he was going to express the normal sympathy one would expect for the widow of an old and close friend. To my surprise he had something else on his mind.

Apparently when he had discovered Henri was suffering from uraemia in 1941 he warned him he would have to give up drinking altogether or he would not live much longer. I had never seen Henri really affected by alcohol but he did love all the good things in life, especially French liqueur brandy, which he drank after every meal.

I appreciated the doctor's confidence and I knew why he was doing it. He guessed how much I would be reproaching myself over Henri's death and, furthermore, he knew that my father-in-law had accused me publicly of having murdered his son.

Henri had never informed me of the serious side-effects his imbibing would have. In any case, I doubt if it would have made any difference. He always said he'd rather be dead than change his way of living. He worked hard and he played hard. He was a *bon viveur*. I think I made him happy. He certainly laughed with me more than he did in anyone else's company.

158

He always said I was like a breath of fresh air.

I was pleased to leave Marseille and return to Paris. I hadn't had a happy time there.

One of the first things I did back in Paris was to visit O'Leary and Tom Groome. They had both survived Dachau concentration camp and although frail, they were recuperating at the Palais Royal, a hotel requisitioned by the British Government.

The British unit at the Palais Royal was called IS9 (AB). It stood for Intelligence School 9, but was also used as a cover for Military Intelligence (escape and evasion). The AB stood for Awards Bureau. Amongst other things they looked after any returning political prisoners who had worked for them. They gave financial assistance if possible and also compiled lists of the British awards that were to be given to their helpers in France.

They had a modest mess and bar and were anxious to obtain reasonably priced champagne, which was extremely difficult to buy. An RAF officer and I were given the task of finding the champagne. We set off in a jeep for Reims. We were able to procure small quantities from several firms well liked by the British and Americans but then I suggested we approach Krug which was the only champagne we served in our home in Marseille when it was available. In those days it was not well known outside France.

The manager was perplexed to see a British outfit interested in his firm's champagne. However, when I explained I was the widow of a Frenchman and that it had been our favourite champagne, he opened the doors wide and we were able to buy as much as we could afford. I was absolutely delighted with our success but my delight was short-lived when we returned to Paris and I heard the bitching and moaning about the 'unknown' Krug.

I was so disgusted I went off to have a drink with a restaurateur friend and told him my sad story. Being a connoisseur of French champagne he immediately offered to swap the Krug with other champagne suitable for British palates. Everyone was happy except the Third Secretary at the British Embassy who had been informed of my so-called disastrous choice. The story told against me misfired as all he said was, 'My God, don't tell me she found some Krug. I'll buy the lot.' However, it was too late. I didn't hear anymore criticisms of my knowledge of French champagne.

Donald Darling, who had been my host in Gibraltar, was the CO of the British Unit at the Palais Royal. We had never had very much in common and although there were some happy and hilarious occasions at the Palais Royal, I was like a fish out of water. As far as I was concerned, the most amusing incident during the months I was there was the night Donald Darling fell flat on his back having been punched on the jaw by O'Leary.

Over the years I have heard a variety of stories about myself — some were true and others were complete fiction. Many of the stories were true except for one detail: they were about other people and had nothing whatever to do with me.

It was common knowledge that I could behave in a very unorthodox manner when I felt I had a point, so perhaps certain people with nothing better to do than gossip, felt sure that I was bound to be the ringleader of any juicy tale that happened. One day in London an air attaché, sitting at my table, regaled the other guests about the day I punched Donald Darling on the jaw. Not one word about the real culprit! I was speechless! It is true that I did punch a man on the jaw in Paris, but mine was a question of national loyalty whereas O'Leary and Donald Darling were having a sordid argument about a female.

My KO happened in the British Officers' Club in Paris just after the Liberation of France. It had previously been the German Officers' Club. Kathleen Hampson and I were dining at the club, sitting at a table near the waiters' servery. She was a good-looking English girl—quiet and distinguished. (She married my brother several years later.) She did not speak French and tended to be slow when ordering her meal. Our waiter was not only impatient, he was also discourteous, and when our order was not forthcoming he muttered under his breath, in French, that he preferred the Germans any day to the rotten English. That was too much for me. I followed him into the servery and delivered a few well-chosen words, followed by a mighty punch on the jaw. He fell flat on his tack, unconscious. I returned to our table and discussed the menu

160

with Kathleen (in English of course).

Then all hell broke loose. Every available waiter arrived on the scene, yelling at me in French, which by this time I pretended not to understand. All through the drama, Kathleen, by the way, didn't turn a hair or give any indication that she had witnessed anything unusual! She just sat there quietly studying the menu!

Suddenly the head waiter arrived and to my horror attempted to revive the waiter with a glass of vintage Bisquet Dubouche (a brandy to which I was very partial). I dashed into the servery, snatched the glass out of his hand, saying 'Ca alors, mon!' and drank the contents. Once more I returned to our table and refused to say another word.

By this time the manager, appeared accompanied by the Third Secretary of the British Embassy who took one look at me and Kathleen and the groggy waiter, and turned on his heels and disappeared.

Kathleen and I dined, served by another waiter, and ambled off to the American bar where it was obvious everyone had been told about the incident. The service was impeccable and then out of the blue Kathleen piped up and said, 'Duckie, I don't think we'll have any trouble with the waiters!'

Much later I was told that the Third Secretary had advised the manager and the waiter to forget the whole affair, adding, 'Do you know that just a few weeks ago this woman was killing Germans who would make mincemeat out of you two?'

It's therefore easy to understand why I was never again given a table near a servery and why that waiter disappeared. Perhaps he joined his friends in Germany.

Hubert had taken up his appointment and as he was to be in London for several months before being posted he asked if I would lend him my little flat which was near his office. I agreed to do so and of course it was given rent free. I didn't hear from him for months but upon returning to London I soon discovered the reason for his silence.

He had lived in the flat while he was in London and on being posted overseas had sub-let it to a colleague of his at the War Office. I telephoned this gentleman who at least had the courtesy to call on me and offer his apologies. Hubert had assured him it was his flat and pocketed the money. A couple

161

of weeks later his mother called and asked when she could take possession of her son's flat as the one she was occupying was too big for her.

People have often asked me what happened to Hubert. I would imagine, if he has any sense at all, he is still keeping well out of my way.

It had been arranged that in January 1946 Colonel Buckmaster would present a Lysander aircraft to the French Government, on behalf of the British Government and SOE. It was to be a memento of the operations carried out by this tiny aircraft between the two countries during the Occupation of France.

At that time I was in a depressed state of mind and refused the invitation to attend the ceremony in Paris. However, Harry Peuleve, a close SOE friend, and Denden came round to my flat and begged me to accept. The celebrations would go on for three days and many exciting reunions had been arranged. They both said it would be good for me. Actually I think they were both worried about me as it was unlike me to be down in the dumps.

They both promised they would find me some gorgeous Frenchman to cheer me up and Denden went as far as to say that if they did not succeed he would put himself at my disposal. The picture of Denden putting himself at my disposal made me roar with laughter as he had never had an affair with a woman in his life. But I agreed to go to Paris, much to their delight.

There was a thick fog over the London area the morning of our departure and we were delayed at our assembly point just around the corner from my flat. As the early editions of the afternoon newspapers came out I thought Denden looked a bit worried. When still another delay was announced he suggested some of us should return to the comfort of my flat until the fog lifted.

Denden had been to a party the night before. He had got carried away and announced that he was the one who was going to present the Lysander to the French Government—and there it was in black and white in huge headlines. No wonder he was nervous and afraid to run into the Colonel in case he had also seen the article. We all knew Denden so we

162

could see the funny side of it. Eventually our flights were cleared and we flew off to Paris.

Food was very short in France so I had purchased a raw goose from a friendly restaurant-keeper in London to take to the Tardivats. It was heavy and by the time we landed it was falling out of the paper wrapping. The first person I saw as I stepped out of our plane was an old friend, Bernard Gohan. Bernard had walked over the Pyrenees with me, and had been cross when he thought I was stingy with my lavatory roll. He had joined the Fleet Air Arm in England but was back with Air France. He couldn't come over as he was waiting to take off but that didn't prevent him from yelling out a few witticisms about bare bottoms and lavatory paper, much to the amusement of everyone within earshot.

Our accommodation had been reserved at a good hotel on one of the boulevards. We were each given the number of our room—mine contained twin beds—and I unpacked. Every now and again Denden would appear, look at the number on the door and then hurry away, mumbling to himself all the time. He came back with Harry and the reception clerk who checked his reservation list to find that Captain D. Rake and Captain N. Wake had been allotted the same room. They had assumed the slight difference in surnames had been a typing error and had thoughtfully put the two 'brothers' in the same room. Denden actually screamed, to the astonishment of the reception clerk, and fled down the corridor as if a whole brigade of Gestapo agents were after him!

There were no official receptions that night so I went over to the Tardivats and returning to the hotel about 3 a.m. I happened to notice Denden getting out of a taxi. I hid in the the shadows and just as he came through the revolving doors I whispered, 'Denden, my darling, I'm waiting for you.' Remembering his rash promise made in London, he bolted and crashed into the glass doors, cutting his forehead as well as breaking one of the doors. Although we gave him first aid treatment, for three days, everytime he took his hat off he removed more skin and his forehead was completely raw. Harry, who was as fond of practical jokes as I was, told him it would have been easier to get it over with and save his skin.

No one in the world can outshine French hospitality at its

best and those days in Paris were no exception. In spite of the difficulties still encountered when catering for large banquets the French had lived up to their reputation.

Although my friends did not find me the gorgeous Frenchman they had promised, I completely recovered from my brief spell of depression.

Taking part in the victory parade in London on 8 June 1946 was a thrilling experience. The atmosphere in the capital during the whole week was electrifying: there was so much excitement and happiness in the air. In spite of the tragic loss of life during the war years one could not quell the exuberance of the fortunate people who had been spared. To watch thousands and thousands of Allied servicemen and women as well as Great Britain's own Armed Forces, and a multitude of civilian services, was a sight never to be forgotten.

The Special Forces manned four jeeps, each one carrying four SOE agents, one of whom was a female; we followed the jeeps of the Special Air Service. The other three girls and I had slept at the Albany Street Barracks the night before as we were due to assemble in Regents Park early in the morning. We were late leaving our starting point and there were delays all along the route the mechanised columns were taking.

We were held up in Whitechapel and when the residents noticed our parachute wings they ran around calling out to their neighbours to come and look at the girl parachutists. In a flash dozens of people came running out and handed us glasses which they kept refilling with beer. It was very welcome as we were all in a delicate state of health owing to the celebrations the night before. We were at the receiving end of some good-natured banter from the SAS boys as we were the only ones getting any attention, or beer.

As we approached the heart of London we could hear the cheering of the crowds and it was deafening. From Parliament Square to Buckingham Palace all the public buildings were decorated with large flags representing both the fighting and civilian services. Along the Mall there were over a hundred masts bearing the flags of the services, dominions, colonies or fighting allies, each one indicating the name of the service or country represented.

The saluting base was opposite Marlborough Gate. We

saluted the late King George VI who was taking the salute, surrounded by the royal family, officials and dignitaries. After the procession came the spectacular fly-past, over a dozen types of aircraft being included in the formations.

The well-known palaces and buildings were floodlit for a week. From ten that night there was a searchlight, aquatic and firework display centred on the Thames between Hungerford and Vauxhall Bridges. There was dancing in the famous London parks to the music of the military dance bands. It had been a wonderful day and a wonderful week was to follow. The city of London had hosted magnificently.

PART FOUR

CHAPTER ELEVEN

Denden was finding it just as hard to settle down as I was. He came to lunch one day with the exciting news that he had been employed by the Passport Control Office and was being posted to their visa section at the British Embassy in Paris. He begged me to apply for a similar appointment, at the same time giving me the name and telephone number of the person who had interviewed him.

I had been endeavouring to find a suitable job but so far no one had expressed any interest in a woman with my background. There were thousands and thousands of men and women in the same boat in Great Britain at the end of World War II. Unfortunately, Britain has never been noted for looking after her loyal citizens once the hostilities are over.

This time I was lucky. My interviewer at the Passport Control Office was a charming and friendly woman—Miss Southam—and within two weeks I was off to Paris to work in the same office as Denden. I would have accepted a posting anywhere but to be actually paid to live and work in my favourite city was the most fortunate thing that had happened to me for some time.

On the whole the staff at the visa section were easy to get along with, especially those holding temporary appointments as Denden and I did. Some of the permanent civil servants took themselves a little seriously and obviously considered they were superior in every way. I was appalled to witness how some of them looked down on our foreign applicants. However, the head of our department, Sir Robert Mackenzie, was one of the most considerate and compassionate men I have ever met and it was a pleasure to be associated with him.

Denden, Ian Marshall and I formed a close-knit little group. We often dined together, discovering masses of little bistros in and around Paris. It was a happy time, especially for me as I could keep in touch with many of my Resistance friends.

Picon followed me wherever I went—even to the toilet; he

would not let me out of his sight. He slept by my desk at the office and knew Paris as well as we did. When he became ill late in the winter of 1947 the veterinary surgeon diagnosed dropsy. I had the liquid drained from his stomach twice. After each operation he jumped up and down and ran all over the place just like a young dog, but after ten days or so his stomach would be bloated again. The vet told me I was being selfish and it was cruel to keep him alive. I had to make a dreadful decision and have him put to sleep—he was just over thirteen years old. I was utterly miserable. The last link with my youthful care-free days of the thirties had gone forever.

The following summer I was posted for several months as a relieving officer at the visa section of the British Embassy in Prague.

Prague may have been an enjoyable city to live in before Hitler cast his eye on the Sudetenland—it was certainly beautiful—but when I was there in 1947, although the Russians were not visible, the majority of Czechs I met used to walk around looking over their shoulders in case someone was listening to their conversation.

The senior passport officer in our visa section was a peculiar man. Unbeknown to me, my war record had reached Prague before I did. He seemed determined to convince me that he had also suffered during the hostilities in Europe. He told me a pitiful tale of the harrowing life he had led when he was posted to the British Embassy in Istanbul. I failed to see how he could have experienced much anguish while being employed by, and under the protection of, the British Embassy there.

He was a naturalised British subject and, strange as it may seem, he went around Prague discussing all foreigners in a derogatory manner. When the Czechs came into our office he tended to look down on them in much the same way as some of our officers had treated the applicants in our office in Paris. I found this attitude in a British subject distasteful, considering the lack of support, moral or otherwise, Czechoslovakia had received from Great Britain, amongst other nations, in the pre-war years when Hitler was installing himself in Europe. I was glad I had only been posted to Prague in a temporary capacity as I hated the atmosphere in our office which was due solely to this naturalised Britisher. He did not know the meaning of the word compassion.

Coming back from lunch one day, I found a man and woman with two little children waiting in the grounds of the villa which the visa section occupied. I was unaware that they had called at the office before the luncheon break but had been sent away by the unsympathetic senior passport officer. When he saw them waiting in the queue that afternoon he asked me to deal with their case. I soon found out why he had palmed them off on to me; first of all, it was a tricky case and secondly, he was hoping I would not be able to cope.

The man had been in the Free Polish Forces and while in Scotland had married a young Scottish girl. After the war the Poles were given a choice of remaining in the United Kingdom or returning to their homeland. Perhaps his wife influenced his decision to return to Poland. She probably thought it would be exciting to see Warsaw, having always lived in a remote part of Scotland. Once they had settled in her husband's country she found the conditions were not as glamorous as she had hoped and they decided to return to the United Kingdom. Then he found he could not obtain an exit permit.

They had walked many kilometres through Poland and crossed both frontiers illegally, eventually reaching Prague. When the children were too tired to walk he carried them, and in removing his coat during the hot midday sun, he had dropped his wallet containing his money and identification papers.

Our unsympathetic passport officer would not lift a finger to help them, because it entailed a lot of extra work and because he did not want to be involved in case the story proved to be untrue. However, I have frequently found that many civil servants who are chosen for their initiative seldom use it. Luckily for that family, I was not worrying about my job or my pension.

I requested permission to see the Ambassador and, after explaining the case, added that I was sure he was a Pole and his wife was from Scotland; furthermore I was 95 per cent certain they were telling the truth. I also guaranteed to refund the Embassy the cost of sending them to England if they were

171

refused permission to land. He allowed me to continue.

From then on it was marvellous to see how everyone tried to help this little family. Our chauffeur and his wife lived in the lower part of our villa and they agreed to look after them until I could arrange their departure. The chauffeur's wife found new shoes for them as their own were falling to pieces. They were given comfortable beds and plenty to eat—they had to remain indoors because we would have been in serious trouble with the Czech authorities if their presence had been discovered. It was almost like being back in France and working for the escape routes.

I typed out a temporary travel permit and covered it with the most impressive official stamps I could find. The Belgian Legation was very helpful and issued a transit visa as we were sending them back via Belgium.

When all the formalities were completed, our chauffeur and his wife drove them to a railway station away from Prague, where they were sure there would be no police control when they boarded the express leaving Czechoslovakia. I had given them a covering letter for the immigration authorities in England. Presumably they arrived safely. I am sure our senior passport officer would have informed me if there had been any repercussions at the other end.

The shortage of food was acute in Prague. As I had diplomatic status I was able to buy little extras now and again at Lippert's delicatessen which was full of imported biscuits, chocolates, tinned meats and fruits, plus a multitude of other luxury items from various European countries. We were given coupons for twenty-eight eggs per month whereas the long-suffering Czechs only received two per month.

As I could only afford one good meal per day, with two on Saturday and Sunday, I determined to make good use of my rations but without the use of a kitchen it was not easy. The hot water service at the hotel was excellent and to my delight I found that if I put an egg in the hand basin and ran the hot water over it continuously for ten minutes it was almost like a three-minute boiled egg.

I did not have any regrets when I left Prague and returned to Paris. Czechoslovakia was an unhappy country. For years it had been riddled with Nazi spies, greedy, unscrupulous politicians and ambitious traitors.

Before I said goodbye to the beautiful city I wandered over the Charles Bridge and made my way to the Russian tank which had been left by the Soviets as a reminder to the Czech people that they had liberated the country from German oppression. Yes, the Germans had gone, but who would liberate the country from the liberators?

The year 1948 in Paris was a very social one for me. French people were recovering gradually from the effects of the Occupation; most political prisoners who had returned from Germany were slowly regaining their health and good spirits; and there were countless reunions and get-togethers to which I was invited. I saw the Tardivats regularly. Poor Tardivat was having a lot of trouble trying to get used to the loss of his leg which had been amputated right up to the thigh. They had a beautiful little daughter whom they wanted to christen Nancy in my honour. The priest pointed out that it would be impossible as it was not the name of a saint. Henri replied that she would be christened Nancy or not at all. Faced with such a truculent parishioner the priest displayed great wisdom and understanding, and so the christening took place.

The late King George VI was ill, so many of the investitures, including mine, were held at the British Embassy in Paris. I saw many familiar SOE faces as I waited my turn to be decorated.

The Americans also organised an investiture with great pomp and ceremony. The guests were entertained by a very good military band prior to the official proceedings. My decoration came as a surprise but was of course appreciated.

The best dinner party of the year was given by Hector, the SOE agent who should have been our link to Gaspard when Hubert and I arrived in France. He had been arrested by the Germans shortly afterwards and spent the rest of the war as their guest in a concentration camp.

During his captivity he had planned the dinner party he would host if he survived Buchenwald. He had thought of everything he was going to have on the menu, right down to the finest detail. As soon as he was declared medically fit he put his plans into action.

He and his wife employed an excellent French *bonne à tout faire* but he insisted on writing all the instructions for cooking and serving the menu on a chart which he hung in the kitchen. He explained to his wife and the maid that he didn't want anything to be served a minute too soon or a minute too late. They humoured him because he had been in captivity.

Denden and I were among the guests invited. (At that stage we were unaware of the drama in the kitchen.) Everything was perfect. The food and the service could not be faulted. It was early in the morning when we returned from Hector's place to Paris, travelling in six cars which were as full as the passengers. I remember I was wearing a beautiful gown from an exclusive Parisian couturière.

Some bright spark suggested we play not cops and robbers but Gestapo and Maquis. Half the cars would be full of Maquisards and the other half Gestapo. When someone shouted 'Gestapo', the Maquisards threw themselves out of their cars, jumped into the culverts on the side of the road and started 'shooting' the Gestapo. After driving a few more kilometres, the roles would be reversed and it would be the turn of the Gestapo to 'shoot' the Maquisards. The performances continued until we reached the Porte Saint-Cloud and the bright lights of Paris.

My dress was in shreds. My shoes and stockings were ruined. My legs, arms and face were covered in scratches. I looked as if someone had tipped a bucket of mud over my head then sprayed me with dead leaves. Denden's appearance was no better than mine. In this disreputable state we collected our room keys with great dignity from the reception clerk at our hotel. The hotel had been requisitioned by the British Government and no remarks were passed by the staff as we wished them all a very good morning. But wow, it had been a dinner party to end all dinner parties.

After our departure Hector turned to his wife and remarked on how perfectly the maid had carried out his written instructions, adding that it had been a wise decision to write them down on the chart. According to his wife there had been one significant problem. Their maid could not read French. Hector was speechless.

Towards the end of 1948 I resigned from the Foreign

174

Office and returned to Sydney. Looking back over the years I am convinced that instead of attempting to resettle in Sydney I should have enjoyed a holiday seeing my family and friends, then gone back to Europe where I felt more at ease. In 1949 Sydney was still a parochial city, especially in the suburbs, and I was too cosmopolitan for such an environment.

Without a doubt the most stupid thing I ever did was to join the Liberal Party of New South Wales and become involved with politics. They used me in the same manner in which they used several men who had distinguished war records. I could accept the fact that the Opposition would attempt to blacken my reputation but I will never forgive some members of the Liberal Party for having gone out of their way to try and belittle me.

When one looks at the trend Australia is taking in the eighties, it's laughable to remember the trivial things I did which upset the Liberals. For instance, my legs were beautifully suntanned so I never wore stockings during the summer months. Nor did I wear a hat. One evening before dinner I was seen in a beer garden with the landlord and my Liberal Party organiser. The Carrs' Park Branch of the Liberal Party stated they would not campaign for a female candidate who drank beer—and they didn't!

Horror of horrors. I crossed my legs when I was sitting on the platform of the Rockdale Town Hall at a women's rally for the Liberal Party. I only crossed them because the stage platform was so elevated I was afraid the audience would see my panties. Some people complained that I spoke English with a French accent.

I was contesting the Federal seat of Barton which was held by Dr Evatt for the Labor Party. I left my pamphlets in some of the wine saloons in the electorate. I did not accept any of the wines offered—I only wanted the customers' votes. The president of the Barton Campaign Committee enquired as to how their candidate's pamphlets had found their way into the wine saloons. When I pleaded 'guilty' I thought he was going to have a stroke, so I begged my brother to deliver my pamphlets. He had been in Changi and on the Burma Road and met a lot of his old POW mates during his rounds. Poor man! Very foolishly he drank wine with them all and was sick

175

in bed for three days. The president of the Barton Campaign Committee had no sympathy or understanding. Brother Stan and sister Nancy were damned forever.

In those days the sectarian issue was deplorable. Being a Protestant I thought it would be polite to visit the Roman Catholic priests first of all. Once more, I offended the Methodist laymen in the area. I couldn't win a trick. In the end I just carried on with the campaign to the best of my ability and to hell with everything else.

Fortunately I eventually found some kindred spirits in Barton. They were wonderful to me and saved my sanity.

Of course there were a few amusing incidents. At an afternoon meeting in front of a huge audience, the president of the Barton Women's Campaign introduced the senator who was the Minister for Social Services as 'Mister', adding that he was well-known in Canberra for his social activities. Her command of the English language could not keep up with her enthusiasm and she had already introduced me as the 'great free lover' of Barton.

It was just as well that I did not win the campaign, although I reduced Evatt's majority of 23,000 to 127 votes. I would never have become a yes-woman. That is the trouble with the majority of politicians; they make promises they never keep and once elected to parliament they are too scared to voice their beliefs and opinions.

After the Federal elections in 1951, I left Australia and returned to England. My departure had nothing to do with my defeat. I could not find a job in accordance with my qualifications. As soon as I unpacked my trunks and settled into my little flat in London, I felt as if a great load had been lifted from my shoulders.

The following year found me on the staff of the Air Ministry in Whitehall, in the department of the Assistant Chief of Air Staff (Intelligence). It was sheer bliss to be working with compatible people once more. No more stabbing in the back, no more sectarianism and no more pettiness and bickering. Five happy years lay ahead. I only resigned because I remarried.

There were many aspects to my job at the Air Ministry. Not only were they interesting but on the whole I was working

176

with men I could respect and admire. Our little unit was involved with the escape and evasion exercises which were being organised in remote areas of England and Wales in the 1950s. The Reserve Units ran several weekend exercises during the year but the main annual one was organised by our department in close co-operation with the Units.

I was part of a team of four who lectured to the Reserve Units on evasion and escape, and also to specialist aircrews who at some time during their flying duties might need this information. I concentrated on the practical side, taking full advantage of my previous experience. We also flew to Bad Tolz in the Bavarian Alps to lecture the service personnel enrolled in the American School of Combat Survival.

The Korean War Truce Agreement had been signed in August 1953. The following year I completed the interrogation reports of the United Nations' POWs, who had been interviewed upon their release from captivity. Too many people have conveniently forgotten the gory details of that war. I have not.

Whereas I had been horrified by the actions of the Nazis in the thirties and forties, now I was sickened by the evidence of a different example of barbaric cruelty. People who uphold and praise communism, and others who would have the world believe that Chinese communism is anymore refined or civilised than its Russian counterpart, should go to their nearest public library and read and digest the sufferings of the POWs in the Korean War.

I read the report of one brave young British soldier who, for several months, had been kept in an iron cage, out in the open irrespective of weather conditions. The cage was so small he had to crouch down all the time. Instead of going to the lavatory the Chinese and North Korean guards used to urinate all over him; and he was unable to go to the lavatory himself— or wash. He would not sign the 'confession' they had prepared. He never gave in. He sang 'God Save the Queen' at every opportunity.

There were countless prisoners who suffered the degrading humiliation of having human excreta rubbed all over their faces. The treatment meted out by the guards was so savage and degenerate that my body turned numb and icy cold as I transcribed the reports from the tapes.

From time to time prisoners did try to escape from the camps but most of the escapes were doomed from the word go. Not only were the men completely run down, they were starving and could seldom obtain extra food for the journey. If they did succeed in escaping, when they were caught the penalty was, at its very best, solitary confinement for several months without sufficient food or water, and in winter without any heat or warm clothing. On top of all this, it was impossible for these POWs to resemble a Chinese or North Korean. If the local population were caught attempting to help them they suffered in much the same way as did the prisoners.

The conditions were absolutely appalling and although several men, and at least one woman, from various countries went on fact-finding missions to Korea, their investigations did not benefit the POWs. If the visitors were communists or fellow travellers they saw and believed what they wanted to. The non-communists only saw what the Chinese and North Koreans wanted them to see. The Russian onlookers were mentioned in most reports. They were always received with great respect and courtesy. Very few Red Cross parcels reached the POWs. According to the Chinese, the American Air Force was in the habit of bombing them in the same way they bombed the prisoners' mail! The United Nations seemed powerless to bring any pressure on the captors and so alleviate the sufferings of the prisoners.

I studied our interrogation report on Colonel Carne of the Gloucester Regiment, better known as the Glorious Gloucesters. It was in two parts and was a long and complicated one which took me weeks to decipher. The Chinese and North Koreans had done everything possible to break his spirit. They had humiliated him in a degrading manner. They were guilty of instigating a series of the most inhuman acts a so-called human could inflict on another. They were fiends. I will never know how he survived—nor how many of the other prisoners did, for that matter.

Apart from the starvation diets, lack of medical treatment, plus the all-round putrid living conditions the POWs had to endure, they were forced to attend political study groups when they would be lectured on the 'crimes' they had committed and invited to sign their confessions. They would hear how the American people were starving to death, how the Soviet Union alone had defeated Germany and Japan, and various treatises on Marxism, or the translation of Russian propaganda. I could go on and on.

I had never at any time believed that communism was the solution to a better way of life, having seen the behaviour of the Popular Front in France in the 1930s and, more recently, the events in Prague in the 1940s. Once I had completed these reports I knew that my original assessment of communism had been well-founded.

I was nominated to write the manual of evasion and escape which was our next project. Following a suggestion by our counterpart in the United States, it was renamed the *Manual of Combat Survival*. It was to be a classified publication and would be of special interest to aircrews who might find themselves stranded in an unfriendly country.

I had been issued with a permanent entrance pass to the War Office in Whitehall and spent some time in their photographic library and archives. One day, while searching for material for my manual, I came across a report on 'Albert' who had been in the O'Leary organisation. To my amazement this report, signed by O'Leary himself, stated that 'Albert' at great personal danger had procured an apartment in Marseille for the evaders. I could not believe my eyes. The danger had been to me, who had found the apartment, been interviewed by the estate agent and signed the lease, and then to my husband who had paid the first six months' rent. I am fond of 'Albert', who did a magnificent job in France, but I was disgusted to see, in black and white, a deliberate untruth, to put it mildly, in an official document.

From then on my clerk and I always kept an eye open for any papers concerning the O'Leary organisation. Consequently I was in a position to read a lot of official material that could embarrass the people concerned.

The manual was duly completed. While it was being edited, I was granted what is known in the Royal Air Force as an 'indulgence passage'. This meant that I was able to enjoy a free return flight to Australia on a service aircraft. I'd earned it. The Pentagon had had five people writing their manual,

179

with a backup team of secretarial help. I worked with one clerk and the general typing pool. The outward journey was by Comet, a new aircraft in those days. I travelled back on a Hastings which stopped in several isolated places and I had a wonderful time both ways.

Our Comet broke down and we waited three days in El Adem in Libya before the spare parts arrived from England. I wondered how on earth I could survive surrounded by sand, flies and mosquitoes—to say nothing of the heat.

One of the passengers on the Comet was a British Army Brigadier. He was on his way to Melbourne to attend a defence conference. He was able to acquire army transport and invited some of us to accompany him to the military cemetery at Knightsbridge, where his brother-in-law was buried.

We all set off after breakfast one morning. It was a very emotional experience to travel over the same territory and tracks that our fighting forces had taken years before—the same places that had been the scene of the bloody battles that had led to ultimate victory. All along the route we took I recognised the names of places that had meant something to the Allies during World War II.

Eventually we reached the British cemetery. I was amazed to see so much green grass in the middle of the desert. It was beautifully kept. The Regimental Sergeant Major in charge had been for years in Egypt and apparently had acquired some special knowledge of growing a certain type of grass which survived the desert and their watering system. Whatever the secret, it had been put to good use here in the cemetery.

Once inside the huge entrance gate one could see the high columns, each one representing the different Allied countries who had been fighting in North Africa. They were interspersed with rows of green grass. The whole area was immaculate and I felt it was a tribute to the RSM and to the men who had lost their lives in the desert.

The French cemetery was a disaster. The Arabs were paid to maintain it and it was obvious the money had gone astray.

We set off for Tobruk, anxious to visit the German cemetery which had been opened not long before by Frau Rommel. We stood outside the main gate and laughed. It was open three days per week and then only for two hours. Fancy going to

Tobruk to find such hard and fast rules.

A desert storm prevented us from going on to Knightsbridge so we spent the afternoon in Tobruk, where a British Army unit extended some welcome hospitality in the form of sandwiches, lovely cold beer and the use of their swimming pool. I was glad I had the opportunity to see the sites of so many battles and so much history. I marvelled at the stamina and tenacity of the men who had fought on our behalf. The price of victory had been high. It had been a long, hard battle but history had been made.

From then on there was never a dull moment. The Brigadier was not a selfish man and when he was given the VIP treatment during our stop-overs, he always included any of the passengers who felt inclined to join his group.

The journey back to England on the Hastings was not as comfortable as the one on the Comet had been, but it was just as interesting. We went via Singapore, Pakistan, Habbaniyalh in Iraq, Cyprus and Malta, but as we remained in each place for several days, there was plenty of time for sightseeing.

John Forward, who was stationed in Malta, was waiting on the tarmac as the Hastings landed. We were both going to attend the wedding of mutual friends in England. The disease must have been catching as we married the week after. I had been widowed for fourteen years and it was a hard decision to make. I had three months in which to decide whether I would remain in the WRAF which I had joined prior to being posted to the Air Ministry. Naturally, I resigned.

I will always remember those years at the Air Ministry with nostalgia. I have always had a soft spot for the Royal Air Force and am grateful for the years I spent in their environment.

Russell Braddon had written a book about me which had eventually been published in paperback and was on sale in all the bookshops in Malta the year I arrived to start my new marriage. As a result of all the publicity we were invited to many social gatherings and in this way we met some charming Maltese. In any case, as far as the Maltese people are concerned, there is a strong tie between their country and Australia, stemming from the First World War. The two years I spent in Malta were happy ones and we were both sorry to leave the island when John's posting had been completed.

CHAPTER TWELVE

This story would not be complete without some reference to 'the film that never was'.

Between 1956 and 1972 there were six attempts to film my story and even the suggestion of a musical. With each offer I became quite excited, and each time I was let down.

At one stage an English tycoon who had an option on my story was unaware that he and I shared a charlady. She noticed some correspondence on his desk concerning Nancy Wake, and told me. I sent her back with plenty of instructions so she could get exactly what I wanted. It didn't take long to find out what a crook he was. After several similar disappointments, I eventually avoided publicity and anything connected with the film world.

But then in August 1972 I received a letter from the English songwriter who'd wanted to make the musical years ago. She was living in California—more questions—more answers—more phone calls. This time there was one big difference—I was invited to California.

There was great excitement amongst my friends in Sydney who gave me a farewell party. We could almost visualise the story on the big screen. There was just one problem—we couldn't agree on the actress who would play my part! I flew off to California, dreaming of the exciting days ahead. I had never remained for any length of time in California and the following weeks were fantastic ones and I enjoyed every minute.

The production company had reserved a magnificent suite for me in a central hotel in Los Angeles. The hotel management hoisted the Australian flag in my honour which created a lot of interest in the immediate area. My arrival at Los Angeles airport was filmed by the camera crew who had been engaged to make a documentary as a forerunner to the movie. Talk-back shows on radio and television had been organised, plus endless interviews.

The next evening the Australian Consul-General had arranged a press conference in my honour at the consulate, and immediately afterwards he and his entourage were invited to a lavish dinner at my hotel. John Alsop and Reeve Schley had been invited. They flew over from the East Coast with their respective wives whom I had not met before. I was in seventh heaven. I adored the activity and found it exhilarating — but then I have always loved the hustle and bustle of the American way of life.

One journalist at the press conference appeared a little belligerent towards me. I gathered he had no time for the French and, in particular, the Resistance. He had also had some unhappy experience in Melbourne and made a few cutting remarks about that city.

When he interviewed me the next day he was pleasant enough. I had not bothered to contradict any of his statements as I knew the production company was hoping for good coverage in his newspaper. He invited me to the opening night of a club that evening. I refused his invitation but when he told me he would introduce me to Lee Marvin and Robert Stack I agreed to go along with our publicity agent.

We met as arranged. He was with his wife and another friend, and after a few drinks I announced my intention of going back to my hotel as there was no sign of the actors he had mentioned. Whereupon he insisted on taking us to the Hideaway Bar in the Beverley Wilshire. I had been drinking whisky all the evening — now he tried to persuade me to drink tequila. By this time he was getting on my nerves although I managed to remain diplomatic. Finally, I guessed his object. He had heard about my capacity for consuming large amounts of strong alcohol and he was anxious, not only to challenge me, but to drink me under the table.

I knew I was having coffee at the City Hall the following morning, lunching with a nice Australian from the Australian Consulate and leaving that afternoon for Carmel. It promised to be a pleasant, relaxing day so I decided to play along with him and teach him a lesson. At the same time this would have the effect of avenging the honour of the French, the Resistance, the city of Melbourne and womanhood in general.

I announced I would join him in a glass or two of tequila

but I refused categorically to have the rim of my glass dipped in salt. The tequila tasted absolutely ghastly, especially as I had been drinking good Scotch whisky. To his obvious delight I was lagging with three full glasses in front of me. Suddenly I remembered my first experience of drinking neat vodka. I used to toss it down and hope for the best. I adopted the same method and before long he was the one with the full glasses in front of him.

After we had consumed two bottles I became aware of the silence around our table. This man was apparently the 'doyen' of the drinking journalists in Los Angeles. An unknown woman was beating him at his own game. I had him exactly where I wanted him. We continued for hours. Finally I rose and said it was time I went home as I had an early morning appointment. I thanked the barman for the 'delicious' drinks, said goodnight to everyone in the bar, somehow walked out to the car and, ultimately, to bed. I had heartburn for hours; my head ached so much I was unable to move it and arrange my hair as I was dressing to keep my appointment. I only had one hat with me—a lovely French silk beret—but I had a matching frock so I wore that outfit. I looked presentable but I felt absolutely ghastly.

To my horror I was not only having coffee at the City Hall, it was followed by a special presentation, and with my hangover I wondered if I could stand up for any length of time. The usual official proceedings were suspended. A man appeared and in front of the audience he unfolded a scroll which he read out in a voice loud and clear. To me it seemed as if he would never stop. But then I was only concentrating on standing up.

As he handed me the scroll, cameras were flashing left, right and centre. Then came the second shock of the day—I was expected to say a few words.

I have no idea what I said. People who saw the ceremony said I looked so shy and demure. How looks can deceive! Maybe I did look shy but that was only because I couldn't lift my head. I signed a big book and lots of people came over and congratulated me. When I read the scroll, which was beautifully presented, it was full of compliments and touched me deeply. As I write this I can see it hanging on the wall—it is one of my most precious possessions. I will always feel humble but grateful for the honour the Council of the City of Los Angeles bestowed on me that day.

While I was standing up at the City Hall, on the other side of town a great drama was taking place. The 'challenger' was flat on his back with an ice-pack on his head. For the first time in his career as a journalist he was unable to go on an important assignment at 9.30 that morning. I was given this piece of news as I was on my way to the Australian consulate to call for my luncheon host. Fortunately he suggested a Chinese meal and some cold beer, which put me on the right road to recovery.

Eventually I heard the whole story from our publicity agent who had been in the plot with the journalist. Actually I must confess I didn't admire either of them—the journalist was much younger than I was (I was sixty at the time)—but as I have a sense of humour I could see the amusing side. Nevertheless, I was happy I had won the contest.

After I had left the bar and gone home the journalist had found it impossible to get up from his seat. He had been lifted up and taken to his transport in a sitting position—rather as if he had been frozen. When they reached their home his wife and friend had been unable to remove him from the car as he was still in this 'frozen' position. They telephoned the PA who had to get dressed and drive to the other side of the city and lift the man into his bed. The PA had just returned to his home and gone to bed, when the wife phoned again for assistance. Her husband did not appear to be breathing. Once more he dressed, drove to the other side of the city and confirmed that the journalist was not really dead—just dead to the world. When he mentioned the fact that he had not slept much that night I told him it served him right for having conspired to play such a dirty trick on a poor defenceless old woman.

During the afternoon the PA went to see how the journalist was faring. He had regained consciousness and said in a feeble voice, 'I don't think I won that one, buddy old man.' When the PA agreed with him, he asked, 'What happened to her?' On being informed of my much-publicised appearances at the City Hall, he said, 'That goddamned son of a bitch!'

The story of our mad contest spread like wildfire around

Los Angeles. The production company thought the interview might not appear in the newspaper, but it did, although it was nothing like the original one. His wife was a journalist. Perhaps she helped him in his hour of need. One thing is sure and certain, Al Stump will never forget me.

Then suddenly it was time to return to Sydney. I was convinced that those energetic weeks in California would lead to something constructive. The last thing the company asked me to do when I left Los Angeles was to look for some suitable terrain in Australia where part of the movie could be filmed. I was given a bottle of tequila as I left the airport. It remains unopened in our kitchen cupboard.

Months went by and the first script arrived. By this time they had scrubbed the idea of a musical and were going to make a straight movie. I didn't know whether to laugh or to cry. My lovely wire-haired terrier Picon had been transformed into a Mexican Rat who drank gin. Picon loathed the smell of all alcohollic drink and used to turn his back on me when I had been drinking.

The scriptwriter had decided that in the film the evaders would travel from safe house to safe house on a new bicycle. I had never read such trash. I worked it out that if we had only had four evaders at a time, and four safe houses (a very conservative figure), we would have needed twelve new bicycles. Four would leave the first house, four the second and third, but who would bring the bikes back from the last house?

I had a mental picture of the administration such a scheme would have involved in real life. I had found it difficult to buy one new bicycle in Marseille; twelve would have been impossible. Would we have been responsible for teaching the aircrews to ride bicycles or would this have been part of their curriculum in England? How would we cope with fifty evaders? How could we have prevented neighbours from being curious to see so much activity and so many new bicycles? But there was more to come.

In the script I had escaped from Spain in a rowing boat and arrived safely in England. It did not mention the route I had taken but presumably they didn't intend to send their heroine through the Straits of Gibraltar. Therefore I must have com-

186

menced my arduous sea voyage from the northern part of Spain and rowed straight through the Bay of Biscay. I imagine the writer had never looked at a map of the world. I had to read all this ridiculous nonsense several times to make sure I was not going mad. I gave up all hope of seeing the film on screen.

More months passed and I received a phone call from London. The action had gone to England and I was invited to go over and meet the new producer. I knew of his father and felt sure he would not be a party to anything underhand.

A room had been reserved for me at the Churchill Hotel for eight days but as soon as I arrived I was invited to stay a further week. I came back from lunch the day the first week was up to find I had been put out of my room. The man responsible for paying the hotel bill was asleep and had asked not to be disturbed. I was absolutely livid and went to stay with friends in the country. I rang the producer that night to explain what had happened and said if they wanted to interview me they would have to come to the country and if they wanted me in London they could send a Rolls Royce.

The producer came to the country the next day (none of this was his fault) and two days afterwards a Rolls Royce was to pick me up and take me to London. I was already waiting for the car when the phone rang. They were finding it difficult to get a Rolls Royce; would a Daimler be acceptable? I said it would.

Not long afterwards my host called out, 'Well, you haven't got your Rolls Royce, Nancy, but there's the biggest bloody Daimler coming up my drive and he's got to keep reversing to get in.' It was a huge limousine and I felt like a dowager duchess as we drove to London.

Through the British producer I was invited to lunch at the Connaught Hotel in London by James Mason and his wife. It was a happy occasion for me as I had long been an admirer of his acting. He was probably pulling my leg when he enquired whether I would prefer Australian wine to the French. I replied that as far as wine was concerned I was not a great nationalist.

When the interviews with the scriptwriter and producer were finalised I spent a few weeks in France looking up old friends before returning to Sydney. A long silence followed all that activity in London to be broken at long last by a letter from the American company stating that the British producer had let them down and the project was abandoned. I didn't believe the excuse they gave; this American crowd always blamed someone else for their failures. They hadn't even had the decency to apologise to me for having forgotten to reserve my room for the second week. I gave up all hope of seeing my story on the big screen and concentrated on more mundane matters.

Several months later another film company in England expressed an interest in the book which led to them taking up an option for twelve months with a possible renewal for nine months. This time, however, there was no feeling of excitement on my part. Enough was enough.

One day I received a phone call from Canberra. The caller wanted my address as the author of a book about Denden wished to contact me. His letter arrived in due course and to my surprise the same corporation who had taken the option on my story had acquired an option on Denden's. It seemed clear they intended to combine the two. I wished the author luck. I felt he needed it as I had read his account of Denden's life when we were together in the Maquis and as far as that period was concerned it was full of inaccuracies which was typical of Denden's way of recounting stories. I had found some of the chapters to be nauseating. I don't know what happened behind the scenes, but the corporation dropped the option. If it had gone any further I would have had a great deal to say.

I had heard tales about film companies which I had not taken seriously. Now I had to admit that most people in that line of business lived on another planet which made it difficult for an ordinary mortal to unravel their intricate system of wheeling and dealing.

Film producers are not the only people who do not know the problems facing safe houses, evaders and escapers. When I had completed the *Manual of Combat Survival* at the Air Ministry a copy was sent to the Royal Air Force Air Attaché in each country concerned. We needed confirmation that the local information I had included in each Manual was up-to-date before sending it to be edited. The Air Attaché in Warsaw replied that I should advise the aircrews that as the terrain in Poland was fairly flat they should steal a horse and cart as this would be an easier way of travelling.

I had visions of the evader arriving at the safe house with his horse and cart. Sometimes in France we had found it difficult to conceal and feed one airman, let alone a horse. On the other hand, I could picture the irate farmer reporting a stolen horse and cart to the authorities who would then be hot on the trail of the evader. Some people have no imagination but I suppose this unrealistic scheme would appeal to film producers.

I had been toying with the idea of writing a book for some time but I didn't think I could write well enough to make it interesting. But then I read a number of books about the Occupation of France and the Resistance—some were good and some were very bad—and I began to think I should put pen to paper. Many screen and television movies dealing with France from 1939 to 1945 have, to my mind, been full of glaring faults. Some lacked a ring of authenticity although they had apparently been produced with the help of expert advice.

I remember in one film about an escape-route network the woman leader gave orders for a pilot to be shot simply because he had the name of a German girl in his address book. Perhaps he had been guilty of some dangerous indiscretion—or even worse—but to shoot him out of hand without first interrogating him would have been stupid. The life of an Allied pilot was valuable; it cost money and time to train them fully. Furthermore it would not have been easy to dispose of the corpse in a village inhabited by naturally curious French people.

In another film a young one-armed man, obviously English, wanted a breath of fresh air so he went for a stroll around the busy port of occupied Marseille. He would have been the most suspicious-looking person in that area and would have been soon picked up. Another character loathed the French and kept saying so in front of his hosts at the same time accepting their hospitality. I don't believe any airmen would have been guilty of such a breach of etiquette. They came from all walks of life and were grateful for the assistance they received.

I have often been embarrassed when reading articles about myself. Frequently they would give the reader the impression that I myself won every battle that was fought in the Auvergne. Of course, that is all tommy-rot. When we were surrounded by 22,000 German troops Denden and I were the only two people not fighting, yet one article stated I had led my 8,000 men to victory. I had a mental picture of myself surging ahead (rather in the style of Joan of Arc) followed by the faithful 8,000.

The truth is we all worked as a team and any success I had was because I was working in harmony with dedicated French people and close friends. I enjoyed fighting with the men when I got the chance but so often I was fully occupied travelling from one Maquis group to another, coding my messages with Roger, listening for the replies on the BBC and organising reception committees for the parachute drops. Another article said I had blown up all the targets on D-day. In fact I was upset because I missed all the fun as I had gone to collect Bazooka from Montluçon.

Thirty-five years after the war I went back to the Auvergne. This time they knew I was coming, and it wasn't by parachute. I will never forget that weekend. It was about eleven in the morning when I arrived at the hotel where I was to stay, in a village which had been known favourably by the Resistance. This particular innkeeper and his wife had been good to us during the Occupation. She was a fantastic cook and was already busy preparing the luncheon which had been ordered by Henri Tardivat in my honour and to commemorate the days we had together in the Resistance.

I went into the little bistro attached to their hotel and ordered a Ricard. Every now and then a dirty face would appear through the beaded curtains hanging on the entrance door, wave a hand and disappear.

By noon all of the men were present, faces no longer dirty, and dressed in their Sunday best. What a reunion. Most of us recognised each other. Some were fatter, some were slimmer, some bald or going bald, but the old feeling of comradeship was still there. We had been linked by our love of freedom and our hatred of the Boches. And we still admired and respected

190

each other even though we came from different countries and walks of life.

The lunch was superb. The odd tourists who happened to lunch there that day probably wondered about the huge table, headed by a solitary woman surrounded by dozens of men.

About three in the afternoon some of us proceeded to the farmer's property where I had landed so long ago. He was sitting on the steps of the kitchen door chewing tobacco. He gave a shout as I approached, stood up, took me in his arms and gave me a big hug and a kiss. Then he turned to his womenfolk who had appeared at the scene, roaring at them to get this, do that; and while they were scuttling all over the place we sat down at the kitchen table. Almost immediately the coffee pot was on the table preceded by the glasses and the *pousse-café*.

Then the reminiscing commenced. While all this was going on the women were standing up and I asked them why they did not sit down. The farmer butted in immediately and said they preferred to stand. I laughed and asked if 'Women's Lib' was unknown in France. When the farmer went out to milk his cows the womenfolk told me they didn't need Women's Lib as they were the bosses even though the men did not or would not believe it. I could well believe it of the country folk because during the Occupation I never once met a farmer who did not confer with his wife before making an important decision.

Once the women and I were alone we sat around the kitchen table and the conversation was very touching and feminine. They took this opportunity to ask me questions of an intimate nature that often puzzle women when they meet a member of their sex who had lived so close to so many men for any length of time.

I told them how London would drop personal parcels for me with the arms and money. There was usually face cream and other little luxuries as well, and sometimes a note from SOE friends.

Looking back at World War II, I think the seeds of the Resistance may have been sown after the Fall of France, but it took most people some time to digest the humiliating details of their defeat. The main danger for all was the ever-growing risk of confiding in the wrong person. I was one of the fortunate ones. I was surrounded by friends I could trust and who never failed me on the occasions I appealed for help.

The Germans had made an astute move when they established Marshal Pétain as the head of the newly created Vichy Government. Throughout France he had enjoyed a huge following since World War I and the Germans used his name to their best advantage. The Father of France image was rammed into us until all but the very loyal (and there were many) were sick of the sight of him and the sound of his name.

There were, of course, many people in France who could have helped the Resistance and failed to do so. There were others who worked willingly for the Germans or the Vichy authorities. There were others who sat on the fence. Thousands were waiting for the day General de Gaulle would appeal for their support. Some would help the Allies but steered clear of their own countrymen. Others would not lift a little finger to help a Jew. Some would denounce them. Hundreds of farmers in the north risked their lives and the lives of their families by helping Allied airmen who had been shot down during the bombing raids.

The Corsican gangsters from Marseille made a mint of money for themselves and the Germans by organising huge black-market and take-over deals. It was not just black market to survive, it was for profit, and the stakes were enormous. In Paris anyone connected with the Germans made money, although they were not always Parisians. It was heartbreaking to witness French people betray their compatriots, sometimes for money and at other times out of spite or jealousy, or to avenge a past grievance. But there are traitors the world over—and in peacetime.

The German propaganda machine worked full-time. They did not miss a trick. They used the French whenever they could. They managed to sow a seed of doubt in the minds of anyone who listened. They were good at their job. They were professionals. It was deplorable to see so many citizens selling their souls and their country for filthy lucre. Thousands of Jews were betrayed but not before they had been fleeced of everything they possessed.

I was only forty-eight hours in Occupied Paris and in that short time I was sickened to see the 'kept women' displaying their finery in the company of their benefactors. Sadly, quite a number of women belonging to French society were also enjoying the favours of the enemy. It was not a happy sight. Some of them paid for their folly but too many escaped punishment after the Liberation. I could go on and on, but it is all so much water under the bridge.

I have not been able to establish the exact percentage of French people who collaborated with the Germans at the expense of their compatriots. Many people were employed by the Germans—sometimes by force—but managed to remain loyal to their country. Some of the wealthy families, afraid for their estates under a communist regime, turned towards the extreme right-wing groups and by the time they woke up to the hard, cold truth of where they were heading, it was too late to retreat.

France has always been hospitable towards refugees and the White Russians were no exception. Yet when the Germans promised to return their estates in Russia once they had won the war, many of the refugees believed the Germans and turned against their hosts.

The formation of the Milice in early 1943 must remain forever a deplorable blot on the pages of French history. They behaved like the savage dogs they were. They were every bit as brutal and uncivilised as the Nazis. They gloried in their work. Several times while I was in central France they drove away in their trucks singing, laughing and shouting with delight, because they had just killed, or burnt alive, some of their fellow countrymen. Too many of them escaped justice.

For my part I will always remember the loyal French citizens with affection and admiration. They faced a heavy penalty for resisting the enemy or for helping the Allied airmen. Yet time and time again, they were there with their support. If they were caught it generally led to a concentration camp or death—or both. It was a heavy price to pay.

I remember the wives of the prisoners of war who were left to fend for themselves those long years; the hunger some people suffered; the bitter winter months with no heating; the curfew; the cunning propaganda in the newspapers and on the radio; the forced labour camps; the turmoil the innocent remark of a child could bring; the horror of seeing family and friends rounded up and shot; the burning of the farms and villages and the people within. Yet in spite of all the atrocities the majority of French people did not collaborate.

The generosity of some French families impressed me many times. People who had very little themselves were willing to share what they had. I collected a young American pilot at a railway station one day. His plane had been shot down in the Champagne area and he had been separated from his aircrew. An old farmer had found him hiding behind a hedge and had taken him home although the area was thick with Germans searching for the airman. The farmer had heard rumours of an escaping network but had no means of contacting them and as the mayor of the village was a known collaborator he was afraid to confide in the local authorities. He and his wife looked after the pilot for over two months when he eventually, through sheer perseverance, found a lead to the network.

Unfortunately, the network could not collect the pilot for ten days and in the meantime it became imperative to transfer him as the Germans began searching all the outlying farms. The farmer, who was not rich, moved heaven and earth to find another farmhouse near their local railway station. He purchased a railway ticket and put the pilot on the train, giving him the instructions needed as he had to change trains twice before he caught the express, which it was hoped would deliver him into my hands.

I had to laugh as the airman stepped off the train. He was dressed in an old-fashioned black and white pin-striped suit. It was probably the suit the farmer had been married in and which he wore to weddings, funerals and christenings. He had a black beret on his head and he was wearing the farmer's gold fobbed watch. He had to know the exact time when he was changing trains and as he only had an airman's wristwatch they had exchanged timepieces.

On arriving at the safe house we offered him a drink. All he wanted was pure water. The farmer had given him French champagne with every meal as he said the drinking water was not fit for human consumption.

The story had a happy ending. After the war the pilot

returned to the farmhouse and to the delight of the dear old farmer, an official ceremony was held at the Town Hall, where the previous mayor was no longer in office.

I am one who believes fervently that the French Resistance played a major role in the Liberation of France. Whatever their shortcomings, they were a permanent thorn in the side of the Germans, thus preventing them from putting all their strength into fighting the Allies during and after D-day. Furthermore, I have no doubt at all that the Allied offensive would not have progressed as rapidly as they did had the Germans not had to contend with the numerous Maquis groups who attacked them continuously from all sides.

In earlier history when groups of people declared war on each other the leaders always led their troops into battle. It is a great pity we do not have the same system today; perhaps our politicians would think twice before they gambled with the lives of their people.

I have been guilty of doing most things high-spirited young people do but to my knowledge I have not hurt anyone but myself. I have been shown the romantic moon from every angle and from a variety of deserts. Inevitably there have been times when cars have run out of petrol in unexpected places. I always accepted a dare when I was young, which was why I entered the kasbah in Algiers at the top end and came out unharmed at the other end to claim my £10.

If I could relive my life I would probably do most things all over again. If World War II had not come along I may have tried to become a good journalist, but I doubt it—I was too romantic to remain unattached. I have never regretted the stand I took against the Nazis. My only regret was the fact that my association with the O'Leary organisation obviously led to the death of Henri. But I realise now that if I hadn't been involved with the escape network I would eventually have found some other worthwhile cause. I could never have submitted to the Germans.

When one remembers all the events in the 1930s which led to World War II, and to the victory which we were promised would bring peace and make the world a better place to live in, one can only wonder if it was all worthwhile. We have only to look around us and see the same thing happening all over again. An old French saying can best express my sentiments. *Plus ça change, plus c'est la même chose.*

*   *   *

In 1984 a Sydney TV channel was thinking of producing a mini-series based on Russell Braddon's book about me. I went to France with the proposed scriptwriters to look over some of the places I'd known during the Occupation, and to try and give them some idea of the spirit of those times.

I'd met the two writers, Moya Wood and Michael Brindley, briefly and I wondered how the three of us would get on in France. As it turned out, we had a wonderful time.

We flew to Paris and stayed there overnight. I took Moya and Michael to meet Micheline Kenny, and we had an agreeable evening in Montparnasse. Micheline had been part of my life for fifty years. I admire her tremendously because she has great courage. Life has not been easy for Micheline, but she always comes up smiling.

I seemed to have lost contact with Madame Sainson after I returned to Australia. I heard conflicting rumours: she had disappeared—she was in New York—she was ill and not expected to live. Then out of the blue came definite news that she'd been seen in Nice. I wanted to write but couldn't remember her address.

Moya, Michael and I left Paris for Nice where Michael had organised a hire car. In Nice we stayed in a hotel in the rue Gounod. For some reason the name seemed familiar, then I remembered it was the street I used to walk down when I went from the station to Madame Sainson's. We found the little street where she lived. Her name was still on the letterbox, and outside her apartment building was a plaque in memory of her husband who had been arrested by the Gestapo, and never returned.

As I knocked on the door my heart was beating fast. The door, secured by a chain, opened slightly and a gruff voice asked, 'Qui est là?' I said, 'Madame Sainson, c'est moi, Nancy l'Australienne.' The door slammed, the chain rattled, and then the door opened wide and after thirty years we hugged each other hard. It was a wonderful moment.

I introduced Michael, who'd come with me, and told her

196

why we were in Nice. All she said was that the TV series was long overdue! Michael raced back to the hotel for Moya, and at 10 a.m. the four of us celebrated with French champagne while Moya and Michael joked about the toughness of their assignment.

Madame Sainson had indeed been to New York, but only on visits to her daughter who had married an American. And she *had* been very ill, but told us that St Peter hadn't been ready for her.

Her apartment hadn't changed, with its artificial flowers still prominent. I'd always teased her about them as fresh carnations were so cheap in Nice.

My little bed was still there—everything I looked at brought back memories of the past; the airmen she'd hidden, so many of them, the good fun and laughter we'd shared in spite of all the danger. We'd both persisted in defying the enemy, and we'd both survived.

We left the next morning for Marseille, where friends had warned me I'd find a big change. They were right—it was ghastly and sordid, the main streets full of shops that looked like cheap Arab bazaars. Everything looked dirty.

We stayed at a hotel on the Vieux Port, and the view of the harbour was spectacular. Michael took pictures of the Fort Saint-Jean where the British had been interned, and the Fort Saint-Nicolas where Garrow had been in solitary confinement. The picturesque stalls where we'd enjoyed all sorts of seafoods had disappeared from the Vieux Port, and had been replaced by Chinese take-aways. We left the next morning and I have no desire to see Marseille again.

Travelling north, we went to Chaudes-Aigues which is a seasonal resort. The hotel we'd lived in in 1944 was closed, but we were made reasonably comfortable in another one nearby. We took pictures of everything—Fournier's house, the hot springs, the river Truyère which I'd crossed after the big battle when we were escaping from the Germans. We went up to the plateau where the arms were dropped by parachute, and to Fridfont and Saint-Martial where Gaspard had his headquarters.

I showed the scriptwriters along the road where I'd been chased by the German plane. One little village had disappeared and although parts of the plateau were now cultivated, everything was easy to recognise. We found the cemetery in Lieutades where Denis had found me sitting on the wall soon after I'd parachuted into France, and we went to Mont Mouchet to take pictures of the monument there which commemorates the Resistance, the Maquis d'Auvergne and Gaspard.

At Cerilly we stayed at the hotel where Tardivat had organised the reunion luncheon several years before. The innkeeper and his wife were still there, and the food was as fabulous as ever.

We went to Montluçon, but couldn't identify the bridge where Hubert and I had been fired on by the Germans when Tardivat had occupied half the German barracks. Then we found the Château de Fragnes, and to my delight the new owner was in residence. Her young grandson was astonished to hear that two men had parachuted on to the front lawn. The chapel was still intact although the organ Hubert used to play was broken in pieces.

Michael and Moya were anxious to retrace my famous bicycle ride from Saint-Santin to Châteauroux. They didn't know how I'd survived the ordeal and, looking back, neither do I.

Unfortunately the Tardivats were in Switzerland, but their daughter Nancy and her family were home when we called. We went to Vichy and took photographs of the monument there which honours all who died for France. It is beautifully kept and surrounded by lovely gardens. I recalled the day in 1944 when I was told so abruptly that Henri Fiocca was dead.

I parted company with the others in Paris, and they went back to Sydney. I stayed a little longer in what will always be my favourite city, where I still have so many beloved old friends.

When I left Madame Sainson in Nice I promised her I would return with my husband the following summer. I kept my word. In spite of her age (85) and ill-health she was a wonderful hostess. We had intended to stay in a near-by hotel but she insisted we be her guests.

Her grandson Alain, who lives in New York, was staying with her for the summer holidays. He enjoyed listening to us reminiscing about the Occupation although he had heard some of the stories from his mother.

Nicole and Claude Sainson had only been young children when I first knew them. Although they had been aware of the intrigues taking place in their home during the Occupation they had never divulged the presence of the evaders. A remarkable achievement for two young children.

Madame Sainson had heard conflicting reports about the whereabouts of the traitor Paul Cole. I was happy to be able to assure her that he was dead and buried. He had survived the war and was living with a lady friend in Paris after the German surrender. Gendarmes making a routine search for German deserters called at her apartment. Cole opened the door, fired his pistol and wounded one gendarme, only to be shot dead by the other one.

The weather was perfect and Nice looked particularly beautiful. The holiday crowds added a happy relaxed atmosphere to the sea-front which we passed on the way to the centre of the town. I took the same route I had taken many times during the Occupation, when followed by several evaders I escorted them discreetly to the photographer.

Everything around me brought back memories both happy and sad. Henri Maffet, my doctor friend in Bar-sur-Loup, and his wife, Raymonde, had been killed in a car accident after I had left France. He had been of tremendous help to me during the Occupation. I will always remember how they both motored over to Marseille in May 1945 so I would not be alone when the end of the war in Europe was announced.

So many of my old friends were dead or had disappeared. For years I had tried to trace Stephanie but I am convinced she is dead, otherwise she would have tried to contact me.

But the biggest blow I received that summer was the death of my old friend Henri Tardivat, after a long illness. It came as a great shock but I had to face reality—I would never see him again. We had been through so much together—so many adventures, so many happy times.

In Paris we stayed at the apartment of Patrick Kenny—that intrepid young voyager of the 1940s! He has a family of his own now but I can still picture him sun-bathing in the little bath tub on the deck of the ship that took us to Greenoch.

Perhaps I haven't achieved what I set out to do over fifty years ago but on the whole I have led an interesting life. Certainly it has seldom been boring.

One thing I have appreciated more than anything else is that the true friends I made over the years remained true friends and to some of them I owe my life. Perhaps I should dedicate this book to all my friends, wherever they may be.

INDEX

'Albert' (resistance worker), 179

Alexander, King of Yugoslavia, 6, 7, 8

Allier, the (*département*), 136, 144, 153, 157

Alsop, John, 138, 139, 140, 142, 148, 150, 151, 152, 154, 183

Anderson, Ron, 93, 94

'Anselm' *see* Bazooka

Armistice Convention, 38

Arnal, Frank, 58, 59, 60, 64

Aurillac, 131–3

Auvergne, the, 114, 120, 123, 130, 131, 134, 137, 157–8, 190; *see also* Maquis

Bachelor, Raymond, 105, 106, 109–10

Barton, New South Wales, 175–6

Basso's Bar, Marseille, 42, 45, 46

Bazooka ('Anselm', René Dusacq), 121–3, 124, 125, 128, 130, 135, 136, 137, 190

Beaulieu, Hampshire, 108, 109

Beaumont, Jimmy, 91, 92

Besalu gaol, 86–7

Bismark (German ship), 49

black market, 145, 193

Bourges, 133

Braddon, Russell, 196

Briançon, 58, 66, 67, 68

Brion, 134

Brindley, Michael, 196, 199

British Broadcasting Corporation, 119, 136, 148, 190

British Expeditionary Force, 39

Broad, Richard, 102, 103, 104, 119

Buchanan, Graham, 126, 127

Buchenwald, 115, 173

Buckmaster, Colonel, 104, 116, 135, 157, 162

Busch, Commander ('Xavier'), 43, 47, 51, 52, 54, 59, 60, 63, 64

Caillat, Pepe, 36

Camargue, the, 18, 19, 20

Canet-Plage, 79, 80

Cannes, 6, 29, 49

Carne, Colonel, 178

Carve Her Name With Pride: see Szabo, Violette

Castres prison, 76, 78

Châteauroux, 131, 132, 133, 134, 199

Chaudes-Aigues, 116, 117, 118, 122, 123, 124, 126, 127, 129, 197

Chevalier, Maurice, 36

Clarke, Captain, 109

Clermont–Ferrand area, 137

Cole, 'Paul' (Sergeant
    Harold), 50, 199
collaborators, 65, 93, 194,
    195
Combined Operations Head-
    quarters, 103
Corrèze, the, 134
Cosne-d'Allier, 114, 138

Dauchau, 63, 81, 159
Darling, Donald, 93, 160
'Denden', see Rake, Denis
Deuxieme Bureau, 16–17
Dieppe raid by Allies, 55
Digard, Andrée, 30
Digard, Micheline, 30, 31,
    47, 95, 96–7, 100, 196
Dowding, Bruce, 47
Dunkirk, 39, 47
Dusacq, René, see Bazooka

Ficetole family, 54–5, 58,
    69, 72, 154
Fidelity, HMS, 48
Fiocca, Henri, 26, 27–8,
    31–33; army call-up,
    37–8; arrest and death,
    51; death, 153–4, 155,
    158, 196; return to
    Marseille, 39; mentioned,
    45, 47, 50, 52, 54, 55,
    56, 59, 60, 61, 63, 64,
    65, 67, 68, 69, 72, 73,
    74, 80, 89, 100, 112; see
    also Wake, Nancy
Forward, John, 57, 181; see
    also Wake, Nancy
Fournier, Henri, 116, 117,
    118, 120–22, 123, 124,
125, 126, 127, 129, 197
Fragnes, Château de, 151–4,
    199
Franco, General, 28
Françoise, 74, 76, 77, 81
Free French movement, 102,
    134, 135; see also Konig,
    General
Free Zone, 39, 49, 71, 78
Fridfont, 127, 128, 197

Gamelin, General, 39
Gaspard, Colonel, 114, 115,
    116, 117, 119, 126, 197;
    evacuation of Vichy, 153;
    battle of Mont-Mouchet,
    128
Garrow, Ian, 48, 49, 50, 53,
    56, 57, 58, 97, 99, 103;
    escape to England, 62;
    Mauzac concentration
    camp, 59, 60, 61, 62, 198
Gaulle de, General, 41, 42,
    43, 51, 102, 192
George VI, 165, 173
Germans, 144, 147, 152;
    migration to Paris, 1933,
    4; compulsory labour force
    (relève), 55, 66, 137;
    surrender, 155
Gestapo, 4, 72, 143, 158,
    197; headquarters,
    Toulouse, 63
Gohan, Bernard, 81, 82, 83,
    86, 87, 89, 163
'Gonzales, Count', 15–16,
    20, 21–2
Groome, Tom, 62–3, 83,
    159

Hampson, Kathleen, 160–61
Hector (SOE agent), 114,
  115, 116, 121, 173
Hitler, Adolph, 3, 4, 16,
  170–71; panzer divisions,
  39
Hodges, Bob (Sir Lewis),
  46–7, 99
'Holy Marys' (Camargue),
  18–19
'Hubert' (British army
  officer), 110, 113, 114,
  115, 116, 119, 123, 136,
  139, 141; mentioned,
  143, 144, 151, 155, 157;
  evacuation of Vichy, 153;
  in London, 161–2

Issoudon, 133, 134

Jean (Spanish guide), 84–8
Jepson, Selwyn, 105
Jews, 3, 4, 41, 49, 51, 193
Juan les Pins, 25, 26

Kenny, Micheline see
  Digard, Micheline
Kenny, Patrick, 199; see
  also Digard, Micheline
Konig, General, 128
Korean War, 177, 178

Langley, Captain James, 98
Laurent (Maquis leader),
  115, 116, 131, 144, 154
Laval, Pierre, 55, 75
Laycock, Sir Robert, 57, 103
Les-Saintes-Maries-de-la-

Mer, 18, 19, 20
Lieutades, 198
London, 1, 17, 30, 101,
  107, 113, 125, 136, 152
Los Angeles, 182, 184
Lourdes, 11, 12

Mackenzie, Sir Robert, 169,
  170
Maginot Line, 39
Malta, 181
Manual of Combat Survival,
  179, 180, 188
Maquis, Maquisards, 55,
  114–55; Americans join,
  138, 146; battle at Mont
  Mouchet, 123–4, 127,
  128; groups attacked by
  Germans, 144; losses,
  130; Spanish group, 145,
  146; *see also* Alsop, John;
  Auvergne, the; Bazooka;
  Clermont–Ferrand;
  Gaspard, Colonel; Schley,
  Reve; Wake, Nancy
Marseille, 6–8, 26, 31, 32,
  33, 35–6, 71; Fort Saint-
  Jean, 45, 48, 197; Fort
  Saint-Nicholas, 53, 56,
  197; Hotel du Louvre et
  Paix, 7, 9, 28, 31, 45, 53,
  154; post-war, 197; Vieux
  Port, 7, 197; *see also*
  Wake, Nancy; World War II
Marshall, Ian, 169
Martinez, Hotel, Cannes, 35
Mason, James, 187
Mauzac, 53, 58, 59, 60, 62,
  63

Merode, Prince de, 80
Mers-el-Kebir, 41
Milice, 40, 71, 76, 132, 143,
146, 147, 193
Montluçon, 114, 121, 122,
133, 135, 148, 149, 150,
151, 198; evacuation by
Germans, 153
Mont-Mouchet, 120, 121;
attacked by Germans, 123;
Resistance monument,
198
Mountbatten, Lord Louis,
103

Nazis, 3, 4, 143, 177, 193,
195
Negre, Gaston, 77, 79
Nice, 54, 82–3, 196–7

Occupation of France, 39,
42–3
Occupied Zone, 38, 102
O'Leary, Patrick, 48, 50, 53,
56, 57, 59, 62, 63, 73,
74–6, 160; arrest, 82,
121; reports on 'Albert',
179; sent to Dachau, 81;
travels with Nancy,
78–80; visited by Nancy
in Paris, 159

parachute drops, 77, 124,
127, 136, 138, 146, 152,
198
Paris, 1, 2, 3, 4, 5, 6, 11, 18,
29; liberated, 152–3, 155;
see also Wake, Nancy
Passport Control Office,

Paris, 169
Passy, Colonel, 102
Pearl Harbor, 53
Perpignan, 73, 78, 79, 82,
83
Pétain, Marshall, 38, 40, 42,
52, 192
Peuleve, Harry, 162
Picon, 5, 6, 31, 49, 58, 73,
83, 154, 170, 186
Pilar (Spanish guide), 84–8
Prague, 170–73, 179
Puy-de-Dome, 115, 133,
144
Pyrenees, 39, 73, 76, 83,
84, 95; see also O'Leary,
Patrick; Wake, Nancy

Rake, Denis ('Denden'), 104,
117, 118, 119, 123, 125,
127, 128, 130, 133, 136,
139, 140, 141, 144, 146,
148, 155, 157, 162, 163,
175; posted to British
Embassy, Paris, 169
Rapley (British Vice-Consul,
Gerona), 88
Ravensbruck, 111
Red Cross, 57, 178
refugees, 12, 38; see also
German migration to Paris
relève: see Germans, com-
pulsory labor force
Renard, Madame, 121–2,
152, 153
Resistance Movement, 37,
40, 43, 44, 47, 51, 57,
65, 72, 73, 191; German
attitude, 121; major role

in liberation, 195; *see also* Busch, Commander; Dowding, Bruce; Maquis; Milice; Special Operations Executive
Reynaud, Paul, 38
Roger (Marine wireless operator), 137, 139, 145, 147
Roger the Légionnaire (French agent of Gestapo), 81, 83, 121
Rommel, Frau, 180

Sablon, Jean, 10
Sainson, Madame, 82, 83, 84, 196–7, 198–9
Saint-Amand, 133
Saint-Hilaire, 149
Saint-Martial, 124, 128, 197
Saint-Santin, 129, 130, 131, 132, 135, 136, 199
Saint-Tropez, 29
Schley, Reeve, 138–42, 147, 150, 151, 183
Scotland, 98, 103–5
Service d'ordre de la Légion, 40
SOE *see* Special Operations Executive
Spain/Spaniards, 11, 16, 153; *see also* Maquis, the
Spanish Civil War, 17, 21, 26, 28, 143, 145
Special Operations Executive (SOE), vii, 103, 104, 116, 134, 151, 157, 162, 173
Stavisky scandals (1933), 27
Stephanie, 5, 8, 9, 10, 17,

18, 19, 20, 29, 51–2, 199; attempted suicide, 21; family in Yugoslavia, 13–15; post-war, 155; *see also* 'Gonzales, Count'
Stump, Al, 186
Szabo, Violette, 111
Sydney, 1, 175, 199

Tarbes, 11, 12, 15, 16
Tardivat, Henri, 136, 137, 141, 145, 146, 148, 149, 163, 198, 199; joins Army after Liberation, 155; leg amputated, 173
torture, 142, 143, 158, 177, 178–9
Toulon, 49, 62, 69
Toulouse, 73, 77, 80
Treacy, Paddy, 74
Tronçais, Fôret de, 141
Truyère River, 129, 197

United Nations Prisoner of War Reports, 177
Unoccupied Zone, 63; Germans enter, 61

Vellat, Dr Pierre, 154, 155
Veterans Legion, France, 40
Vichy, 144, 153; monument to war dead, 199; police, 72, 75
Vichy Government, 48, 192
Vienna, 4, 5, 12

Wake, Nancy:
leaves Australia, 1; life in Paris, 1930s, 3–5, 6,

10–11, 12, 15–16; 20–22; 26–8, 29–30; visits Vienna, 4, 5, 12; visits Yugoslavia, 13–15; marries Henri Fiocca, 31–3; life in Marseille, 35–6, 52; chalet in Nevache, 52, 54, 58; drives ambulance, 38; travels as courier for Resistance, 49, 51, 60, 63, 64–6; as 'White Mouse', 63, 68–9, 72; escapes from France to London: arrest in Toulouse, 11, 73–4; crosses Pyrenees, 76–85; in Spain, 85–93; voyage from Gibraltar, 93–7; arrives in London, 98; trains for SOE, 103–13; parachutes into France, vi, 114; works with Maquis as SOE agent, 114–55; code names, 87, 113, 128; death of Henri Fiocca, 154, 155, 158, 199; tours France with Col. Buckmaster, 157–8; returns to Paris for victory celebrations, 162–3; in Victory Parade, London, 164; at British Embassy, Paris, 169; posted to Prague, 170–73; returns to Sydney post-war, 175; joins Liberal Party of NSW, 175–6; contests Federal seat of Barton, 175–6; returns to England (1951), 176; works at Air Ministry, London, 176–81; granted Indulgence Pass, RAF, 179; joins WRAF, 181; marriage to John Forward, 181; publication of Russell Braddon book, 181; lives in Malta, 181; experiences of film-makers, 183–90; returns to Auvergne (1980), 190; returns to scenes of wartime France (1984), 197, 200

Walker, Captain, 109, 110
war cemeteries, Libya, Tobruk, 180
Wood, Moya, 196, 197, 199
Wellington, New Zealand, 1, 32
Weygand, General, 39
'White Mouse' see Wake, Nancy
Wilkins, Leslie (Wilkie), 46, 99
World War II, 30, 31, 35, 180; British attack on French fleet, 40–41; collapse of French army, 38; German Occupation, France, 39; see also Dunkirk

'Xavier' see Busch, Commander

Ygrande, 136, 137, 138